W9-AGI-112

PHILIP II and
ALEXANDER THE GREAT
Unify Greece
in World History

Don Nardo

Enslow Publishers, Inc.

40 Industrial Road   PO Box 38
Box 398   Aldershot
Berkeley Heights, NJ 07922   Hants GU12 6BP
USA   UK

http://www.enslow.com

Library of Congress Cataloging-in-Publication Data

Nardo, Don, 1947–
    Philip II and Alexander the Great unify Greece in world history / Don
Nardo.
       p.   cm. — (In world history)
    Includes bibliographical references and index.
    Summary: Describes the efforts of Philip II of Macedonia and his son,
Alexander the Great, to unify the different parts of Greece and to
establish a vast Greek empire.
    ISBN 0-7660-1399-5
    1. Philip II, King of Macedonia, 382–336 B.C.—Juvenile literature.
2. Alexander, the Great, 356–323 B.C.—Juvenile literature. 3. Greece—
History—Macedonian Expansion, 359–323 B.C.—Juvenile literature.
4. Greece—History—Macedonian Hegemony, 323–281 B.C.—Juvenile
literature. 5. Militarism—Macedonia—History—Juvenile literature.
[1. Philip II, King of Macedonia, 382–336 B.C. 2. Alexander, the Great,
356–323 B.C. 3. Kings, queens, rulers, etc. 4. Greece—History—
Macedonian Expansion, 359–323 B.C.] I. Title. II. Series.

    DF233.2.N37   2000
    938'.107—dc21   99-037004

Printed in the United States of America

10 9 8 7 6 5 4 3 2

To Our Readers: We have done our best to make sure all Internet addresses in this
book were active and appropriate when we went to press. However, the author
and the publisher have no control over and assume no liability for the material
available on those Internet sites or on other Web sites they may link to. Any
comments or suggestions can be sent by e-mail to comments@enslow.com or to
the address on the back cover.

Illustration Credits: Christine Nelson-Nardo, pp. 11, 26, 33, 37, 50, 58,
62, 79, 80, 97; Corel Corporation p. 7; D. Nardo, after G. P. Stevens, p.
14; D. Nardo, after M. Andronicos, p. 83; Enslow Publishers, Inc., pp. 71,
89; J. G. Heck, *Heck's Pictorial Archive of Military Science, Geography and
History* (New York: Dover Publications, Inc., 1994), pp. 31, 52, 90, 94.

Cover Illustration: © Digital Vision Ltd.

Contents

Chapter 1

The Elusive Dream of Greek Unity

Under King Philip II of Macedonia and his son, Alexander III, later called "Alexander the Great," in the mid-330s B.C., most of the states of ancient Greece achieved a unity they had never before known. This unity was largely the result of Philip's stubborn and tireless efforts over the course of the preceding three tumultuous decades. After transforming Macedonia, long a culturally backward and militarily weak kingdom on the northern edge of the Greek world, into a mighty nation, Philip used a shrewd combination of diplomacy and brute force to bend the cultured city-states of southern Greece to his will. The Greek solidarity imposed by Philip was shaky and did not last long. But its brief existence allowed Alexander, in the decade following his father's untimely death, to carve out the largest empire the world had yet seen and to spread Greek culture throughout the eastern Mediterranean and much of western Asia.

Philip's unification of Greece, however brief, was an achievement of immense proportions, considering the Greeks' long history of mutual distrust and disunity. The Greeks referred to their land as Hellas and to themselves as Hellenes. The idea of all Greeks banding together was known as Panhellenism. To most ancient Greeks, the Panhellenic ideal was an alien and elusive concept. At first glance this might seem odd, considering that modern Greece is a single nation inhabited by a single people. However, although all ancient Greeks shared the same language and religion, their land was physically divided into hundreds of small city-states, each of which saw itself as a separate nation.

The Greeks called the city-state the polis (plural is poleis). Each polis—usually made up of a central town surrounded by supporting villages and farmlands—had its own government, laws, customs, and national goals. Among the most powerful and influential of the classical Greek poleis were Athens, master of the wedge-shaped eastern peninsula of Attica; Thebes, the leading city-state in Boeotia, the region directly north of Attica; and Sparta, located in the southern part of the Peloponnesus, the large peninsula that makes up the lower third of Greece.

On the one hand, the evolution of the polis greatly benefited the Greeks in certain ways, the most important being the development of the concept of individual city-states. The fact that each state was culturally unique, politically independent, and free to choose its own destiny eventually gave rise to revolutionary notions of political freedom and citizen participation in government. In other lands, kings and small groups of privileged nobles dominated poor peasant populations. The Greeks had kings, too, at first. But over time, most city-states threw out these

Zeus, leader of the Greek gods. Although politically separate, the Greek city-states were culturally united in their common religion.

7

rulers and began experimenting with new forms of government that incorporated the concepts of personal freedom and citizens' rights. This trend culminated in the late sixth and early fifth centuries B.C. with Athens' establishment of the world's first democracy. Many other poleis eventually followed suit, adopting democratic ideals of one form or another. (The major exception was Sparta, which retained a form of kingship.) Another advantage of the polis concept was that, in compact societies with small populations, it was easier for able citizens to rise to important positions in which their talents benefited everyone.

Unfortunately, these advantages were often outweighed by the one major drawback of Greece's built-in political fragmentation—continuous rivalries among the various states. As Greek historian M. B. Sakellariou put it, each polis

> sought to expand at the expense of the others; those which gained the ascendancy established oppressive hegemonies [domination] over the rest; the victims of aggression stopped at nothing to protect their integrity, their autonomy, their very existence. All this warring caused serious loss of life and destruction of property, resulting in increasing poverty which was the main cause of the wars. In short, Greece was trapped in a vicious circle of suffering.[1]

Indeed, one generation after another witnessed numerous wars among neighboring city-states or ever-shifting coalitions of these states all across mainland Greece, the many islands of the Aegean Sea, and

Ionia, the strip of Greek settlements along the western coast of Asia Minor (modern-day Turkey).

It must be noted that, during the many centuries of strife, there were occasional calls for and attempts at unity among the Greek states. In 480 B.C., for example, the mighty Persian Empire, based in what is now Iran, launched a massive invasion of the Greek Aegean sphere. Faced with the prospect of annihilation or subjugation, many Greek poleis, led by the two strongest—Athens and Sparta—formed a united front against the invaders. But this alliance was only temporary. Once the Persians had been defeated, the Athenians, Spartans, and many other Greeks almost immediately resumed squabbling with one another. After five subsequent decades of political intrigues, name-calling, and sporadic battles, the Greek world exploded in the disastrous Peloponnesian War. It lasted twenty-seven grueling years, caused untold misery, death, and destruction, and ruined or exhausted nearly all the city-states.

Another call for unity came in 392 B.C., twelve years after the end of the terrible conflict, from the Greek orator Gorgias. Having lived in many different poleis, Gorgias had a unique Panhellenic outlook. It disturbed him that some city-states, seemingly having failed to learn the lesson of the great war, had again begun to fight among themselves. He advocated that the Greeks stop their incessant rivalries and unite in a common effort against their old enemies—the Persians. To dramatize his point, he made his most impassioned speech for unity at the Olympic Games, in which all Greeks competed together peacefully every four years regardless of their differences.

Other orators took up this same theme in the years that followed. Among them was Gorgias's pupil, Isocrates. In his *Panegyricus*, composed in 380 B.C., Isocrates stated:

> It is not possible for us to cement an enduring peace unless we join together in a war against the barbarians [non-Greeks; in this case, the Persians], nor for the Hellenes to attain concord until we wrest our material advantages from one and the same source and wage our wars against one and the same enemy. When these conditions have been realized, and when we have been freed from the poverty which afflicts our lives—a thing that breaks up friendships, perverts the affections of kindred into enmity, and plunges the whole [Greek] world into war and strife—then surely we shall enjoy a spirit of concord, and the good will which we shall feel towards each other will be genuine.[2]

For decades, in essays and letters, Isocrates appealed to the repeatedly warring Greek states to settle their differences. He always emphasized that unity would bring them strength, an end to suffering, and the beginning of untold prosperity. But none of the leaders of those states listened to Isocrates any more than they had listened to Gorgias or the other past voices of Panhellenism.

None of them, that is, except Philip of Macedonia. Having failed to persuade the citizen assemblies of the classical city-states of southern Greece, the persistent

Isocrates preached his Panhellenic ideal to the leaders of less-cultured states on the fringes of the Greek world, among them Philip. For reasons we can only guess, the idea of leading a united Greece to the glorious conquests of other lands struck a chord with Philip. Exploiting Macedonia's large human and material resources and his own considerable talents as a leader, he managed to forge a grand Greek alliance for that purpose.

Thus, Isocrates saw Philip (and Philip likely saw himself) as a unifier, a strong leader who could bring

Olive trees line this gorge in northern Thessaly, near one of the areas seized in 369 B.C. by Macedonia's Alexander II, eldest brother of Philip II.

the constantly bickering city-states together for a greater purpose. The leaders in most of those states saw it differently, of course. Most of the information about Philip that has survived from this period comes from his opponents' documents and speeches. To them, Philip was an uncouth and uncultured conqueror who threatened their independence and way of life. There was probably an element of truth in each of these views. Perhaps Philip is best described as a leader who had not only constructive plans for Greece but also had no qualms about using force to carry out those plans.

Philip did not live to lead the anti-Persian crusade. He was assassinated, and the leadership of the Panhellenic alliance passed to his equally talented son. Ironically, Alexander himself ended up dying prematurely, leaving many of his own plans and dreams unfulfilled. Yet for one brief but shining historical moment, Philip and his son fulfilled Isocrates's Panhellenic dream beyond the old orator's wildest expectations.

Chapter 2

An Inability to Get Along

At the dawning of the fourth century B.C., a century that Philip and Alexander would come so profoundly to shape, the classical city-states of central and southern Greece lay largely shaken, ruined, and exhausted. A mere four decades before, Athens had stood at its magnificent height of naval power and cultural glory. Under a succession of capable statesmen-generals, most notably the remarkable Pericles, Greece's richest and most populous polis had marshaled many of the smaller city-states in the eastern Mediterranean sphere into a powerful maritime empire. Using the vast sums of money that flowed into its treasury from the member states, Athens began a large-scale building program. This effort culminated in the building of the sacred structures atop the city's central hill—the Acropolis—including the Parthenon, the huge, splendid temple dedicated to Athens' patron deity, Athena, goddess of wisdom and war. "Future ages will wonder

13

at us," Pericles conceitedly yet correctly predicted, "as the present age wonders at us now."[1]

But Athens' proud moment turned out to be short-lived, due largely to a character flaw it shared with other Greek states—its inability to get along with its neighbors. The Athenians were constantly at odds with one or more of the "allies" that made up their empire. Treated more like subjects than friends, many of the city-states rebelled. Athens resorted to threats and force to keep its empire intact. At the same time, the Athenians engaged in rivalries and wars with their

The Parthenon, crowning jewel of Athens' Acropolis, as it appeared in its original glory. Macedonian kings, including Philip and Alexander, looked on such cultural achievements with wonder and envy.

traditional enemy, Sparta, which had its own confederation of allies. Most of these allies, like Athens' subject poleis, were kept in line by intimidation. The Spartans had little trouble imposing their will, for although Athens controlled the seas, Sparta had the most effective and feared land army in all Greece.

It was perhaps inevitable that all-out war would erupt between these two rival blocs of poleis. The spark of what came to be known as the Peloponnesian War kindled in 431 B.C. It quickly escalated into a horrific inferno that drew in nearly every Greek state and colony, devastated many, and, after almost three decades, exhausted all involved. Athens had the farthest to fall, and it fell hard. Forced to surrender in 404, the distraught Athenians saw their cherished democracy dismantled and replaced by a Spartan-backed autocratic council. Shortly afterward, Athens was able to restore its democratic institutions, but the incredible energies that had driven its golden age in the preceding century had been drained. Like so many other poleis, Athens had become only a shell of its former self.

Unfortunately, the Greeks seemed doomed to repeat their mistakes. Even after their past rivalries had caused so much suffering, most still stubbornly held on to their mutual suspicions and petty jealousies. Panhellenic unity remained an elusive dream. Less than a decade into the new century, fresh rounds of bickering and fighting began. This only further exhausted and weakened the war-weary cities, leaving them open to intervention and domination by an outside power. Persia seemed the most likely threat. Orators such as Gorgias loudly demonized the empire that had more than once attempted to subjugate Greece. At the time, no one could have guessed that the threat would come from much closer to home. The power that would eventually bring the classical states to their knees would spring from the then-disunited and uncultured Macedonian tribes in the far north.

The Formidable Spartan Phalanx

Thus, the speech that Gorgias delivered at the 392 B.C. Olympic Games, in which he called for the Greeks to unite against the Persians, fell on deaf ears. A great Panhellenic crusade was an idea whose time had not yet come. But some Greeks did support limited attacks on Persia, or more precisely, Asia Minor, which then made up only the tiny westernmost edge of the vast Persian realm. Some of the Greek cities of the Ionian coastal region were under Persian control and others feared attack by the Persian king. Liberating or protecting these cities seemed a worthy venture for Greece's strongest power, which at this time was Sparta. Since their victory over the Athenian empire in the great war, the Spartans had taken firm control of Greek affairs. Sparta's new king, Agesilaus, decided to aid the Ionian Greeks, although this was probably only the official reason for the expedition. His real motives were likely Persian gold and personal glory.

Agesilaus had every reason to believe that he could easily defeat both Persians abroad and fellow Greeks at home. Sparta's army, led by its mighty phalanx of hoplites, seemed just as fearsome and invincible as it had for more than a century. A Greek hoplite was a heavily armored infantry soldier who bore a round shield, the *hoplon*, and fought with a six-foot-long spear and a short sword. The phalanx was an infantry formation that all Greek armies had used since the eighth century B.C. Military historian Peter Connolly explained:

> The phalanx was a long block of soldiers several ranks deep. There were usually eight ranks, but there could be as few as four, or many more than eight. The phalanx was organized in files (lines from front to back) so that when a man fell his place was taken by the man [in the file] behind. . . . The phalanx would be drawn up in open order with 1.5 to 2 meters [about 5 to 6 feet] per man, or doubled up to form close order.[2]

The Spartan phalanx, made up of tough, well-trained, and highly disciplined troops, was so formidable both in reputation and in fact that it either crushed or scared off all opposing armies.

Dissension Among the Greeks

Agesilaus soon learned to his dismay, however, that a nation often needs more than just military prowess to succeed. Although he was a tough, capable general in command of a crack force of troops, he badly overstretched Sparta's resources by trying to raid Asia Minor and run Greece at the same time. The Spartans were far less competent in political affairs than they were in war. They were usually autocratic, inflexible, slow to make decisions and even slower to act on them, and reluctant to stray far from home. Their bully tactics and inefficiency had won them more enemies than ever. Not long after the king and his army crossed over into Asia in 396 B.C., the other Greeks began to plot against him. Persian leaders, obviously concerned about the Spartan incursion into their lands, secretly paid several of the Greek poleis to form an anti-Spartan alliance. Athens, with its newly restored democracy, was only too happy to take the lead against its old enemy. It soon had the backing of two of Sparta's former allies—Thebes and Corinth, the latter located in a strategic position on the Isthmus of Corinth, the strip of land connecting the Peloponnesus to the rest of Greece.

After Agesilaus learned about the enemy coalition in 394, he promptly led his men across the Hellespont (now the Dardanelles, the narrow strait separating Thrace, the northeastern region of Greece, from Asia Minor) and back into Greece. On the way, he received the bad news that an Athenian admiral named Conon, backed by Persian ships and money, had just destroyed the Spartan fleet near Cnidus in southwestern Asia Minor. The frustrated and enraged Spartan king pushed on. Eventually, he confronted a hastily assembled confederate army of Athenians, Thebans, and others at Coronea in western Boeotia. Once more, the Spartan phalanx proved both terrifying and lethal. Seeing the Spartan hoplites, in characteristic red cloaks, bearing down on them, some of the confederates turned and fled without striking a blow, leaving their allies to face the enemy alone. The Greek historian Xenophon, who fought that day in the Spartan ranks, later wrote:

> First, the two armies advanced towards each other in total silence; but when they were about two-hundred yards apart the Thebans shouted out their war-cry and ran in at the double. Then, when there was still about a hundred yards between the armies, from the phalanx of Agesilaus came running out the troops under Herippidas [a Spartan commander]. . . . [Later, Agesilaus and more of his troops] crashed into the Thebans front to front. So with shield pressed against shield they struggled, killed and were killed. In the end some of the Thebans broke through to Mount Helicon, but many others were killed on their way there.[3]

Though the Spartans won the battle at Coronea, their opponents fought bravely and stubbornly enough to make the margin of victory a narrow one. Thus, the anti-Spartan poleis grew bolder and even more defiant. The following year, the Athenians boldly rebuilt their Long Walls, the defensive perimeter linking Athens with its port town of Piraeus, a barrier the Spartans had forced them to tear down at the end of the great war.

Sparta's Leadership Is Severely Tested

The new round of warfare, largely aimed at ending the Spartan domination of Greece, would carry on for many years. The first major blow to Sparta's pride after its embarrassing naval loss at Cnidus occurred in 390 B.C., when a small unit of about six hundred Spartan hoplites passed near Corinth on their way south. Suddenly, the city gates opened. Out rushed Athenian General Iphicrates at the head of a battalion of peltasts. A relatively new addition to Greek warfare, these fighters wore no armor. Each carried only a small wicker shield, and some threw spears. They had no chance in close-order battle against the metal wall of a phalanx. But Iphicrates believed that, when properly trained and organized, swift and agile peltasts might do significant damage to hoplites, whose heavy armor hampered their speed and maneuverability. To test his theory, he ordered a direct attack on the Spartan unit, a tactic until then unheard-of. Sure enough, the peltasts inflicted heavy losses on the surprised Spartans. This incident, though seemingly trivial at the time, marked an important turning point in Greek military science. The potential for combining such lightly armed troops with regular infantry against an enemy phalanx was not lost on Philip. He would later exploit the concept most effectively.

The Athenians and Corinthians were not the only Greeks who tested the Spartans' patience and fortitude. After their loss at Coronea, the Thebans grew increasingly resentful of the Spartans. In the mid-380s, Sparta, wary of Thebes' growing power at the head of a confederacy of Boeotian poleis,

Source Document

And now as the javelins were hurled at them, some of the Spartans were killed and some wounded. . . . The polemarch [Spartan commander] then ordered the infantry in the age groups 20 to 30 to charge and drive off their attackers. However, they were hoplites pursuing peltasts at the distance of a javelin's throw, and they failed to catch anyone, since Iphicrates had ordered his men to fall back before the hoplites came to close quarters. But when the Spartans . . . turned back again from the pursuit, Iphicrates' men wheeled round, some hurling their javelins from in front while others ran up along the flank, shooting at the side unprotected by the [Spartans'] shields.[4]

The term peltast *came from the* pelta, *the wicker shield carried by these troops. The peltasts originated in Thrace. They carried javelins for weapons, which they threw at the enemy and then ran away. When the Athenian General Iphicrates led his peltasts against a small Spartan phalanx in 390 B.C., he showed that they could be lethal against heavy infantry. Xenophon wrote of this incident in his* Hellenica.

demanded that the Thebans break up the alliance. At first Thebes refused, but in time it saw no choice but to comply; its hatred of Sparta increased. Making matters worse, in 382, a group of pro-Spartan Theban politicians conspired with the Spartan commander Phoebidas, whose troops seized the Cadmea, the fortress atop Thebes' central acropolis. Seething at the presence of the enemy occupation force, the Thebans languished in humiliation.

Four years later, however, the tide began to turn against the tough but overconfident Spartans. Two remarkable Theban leaders arose whose courage and inventiveness not only altered the course of Greek history but also forever changed ancient warfare. First, the Theban patriot Pelopidas led a group of soldiers disguised as women into the Cadmea. They killed the Spartan leaders, after which other Thebans stormed the citadel and expelled the occupiers. Then, Thebes boldly reorganized its Boeotian alliance with Pelopidas as supreme commander.

The Fatal Encounter at Leuctra

Pelopidas was a talented cavalry commander, but he knew that the Thebans needed more than his horsemen to stand up to the Spartans, who would surely send their dreaded phalanx against them. So he called on a close friend, the statesman-general Epaminondas, to prepare the Theban phalanx. One of the most brilliant military strategists the Western world had yet produced, Epaminondas carefully studied the traditional way Greek generals used their infantry. He noted that most placed their best troops on the right wing. When two opposing phalanxes crashed head-on, the right wing of the army with the strongest troops usually mauled the enemy's weaker left wing. It then moved behind the other army's right wing, destroying it. If the Thebans met the Spartans in the usual manner, Epaminondas realized, his troops would surely be defeated. His innovation was to draw up his phalanx at an angle, leading with his left wing instead of his right. He would then hit the enemy's right wing, its strongest point, with irresistible force. He made his left wing fifty rows deep, as compared with the Spartans' twelve rows. Epaminondas also trained an elite group of three hundred crack troops, the Sacred Band, to lead the advance.

The encounter came in 371 B.C. near Leuctra, ten miles southwest of Thebes. The Spartan Army under King Cleombrotus was marching toward the city, bent on subjugating it. Epaminondas's plan succeeded with brutal efficiency. As the phalanxes neared each other, Pelopidas led the Sacred Band in a charge at the Spartan right wing. The massive Theban left wing followed. According to the ancient Greek historian Plutarch,

> When Epaminondas' main phalanx bore down on them alone [the soldiers in the Spartan right wing] and ignored the rest of their army, and Pelopidas with a charge of extraordinary speed and daring had already hurled himself upon them, their spirit faltered . . . and there followed a rout and a slaughter of the Spartans such as had never before been seen.[5]

Source Document

By arranging his phalanx in oblique formation, he [Epaminondas] planned to decide the issue of the battle by means of the wing in which were the élite [troops of the Sacred Band and Thebes' other strongest fighters]. When the trumpets on both sides sounded the charge and the armies simultaneously with the first onset raised the battle cry . . . they met in hand-to-hand combat, [and] at first both fought ardently and the battle was evenly poised; shortly, however, as Epameinondas' men began to derive advantage from . . . the denseness of their lines, many Peloponnesians began to fall. For they were unable to endure the weight of the courageous fighting of the élite corps. . . . Now as long as King Cleombrotus of the Lacedaemonians [Spartans] was alive . . . it was uncertain which way the scales of victory were inclined; but when . . . [he] perished in an heroic resistance after sustaining many wounds, then, as masses of men thronged about his body, there was piled up a great mound of corpses. . . . The Lacedaemonians were with great difficulty forced back; at first, as they gave ground they would not break their formation, but finally, as many fell and the commander who would have rallied them had died, the army turned and fled in utter rout. . . . The highest praises were accorded the general Epaminondas, who chiefly by his own courage and by his shrewdness as a commander had defeated in battle the invincible leaders of Greece.[6]

The first-century B.C. Greek historian Diodorus Siculus described the battle at Leuctra, which ended Sparta's domination of Greece.

Though most of the troops in the Spartan right wing fought with their usual skill and valor, their ranks soon crumbled under the Theban onslaught. Their comrades in the left wing fell into disorder. At the battle's end, a thousand Spartans, including Cleombrotus, lay dead. The Boeotians had lost just forty-seven men. In a single stroke, Thebes had forever shattered the myth of Spartan invincibility. The Spartan domination of Greece was over and that of Thebes had begun.

News of the Spartan disaster at Leuctra struck Greece like a thunderbolt from its chief god, Zeus. Sparta's Peloponnesian allies, who had long been kept in line at spear-point, immediately proclaimed their independence. Less than a year after the decisive battle, the urban areas of Arcadia, the region encompassing the central Peloponnesus, defied Sparta by founding Megalopolis (meaning "great city") in the peninsula's geographic center. Agesilaus tried to intervene, but the days of the Spartan bully were over. On four occasions over the next eight years, the Theban Army descended into the Peloponnesus to keep Sparta in line. These expeditions culminated in 362 in a major battle at Mantinea, in central Arcadia. There, Epaminondas's lethal new war machine delivered the Spartans another humiliating defeat.

Trouble in the North

Thebes' sudden rise to a predominant position in Greek affairs occurred when some of the formerly weak and backward northern Greek states were beginning to flex their military and political muscles. Shortly before the showdown at Leuctra, Jason, tyrant of the city of Pherae in Thessaly, the large fertile region sandwiched between Boeotia and Macedonia, united most of the Thessalian clans. Possibly inspired by the speeches of Gorgias, Isocrates, and other Panhellenists, Jason dreamed of becoming the most powerful man in Greece and of leading the united cities against Persia. In this regard, he must be seen as the direct precursor of Philip and Alexander. Jason

Alternating patches of cultivated crops and wild vegetation stretch to the horizon in this modern view of the Macedonian lowlands. The area has changed little since ancient times.

certainly showed potential as a military strongman. He was skilled at siege warfare, and Thessaly had the largest and finest cavalry units in all Greece. However, Pherae's tyrant was assassinated in 370 before he could realize any of that potential.

Jason was succeeded by his nephew Alexander, who was a cruder, more brutal, and far less talented man. Many of the Thessalian clans disliked their new ruler. While he struggled with them, another Alexander appeared on the scene. Alexander II, the new king of Macedonia and Philip's eldest brother, had decided to take advantage of his neighbors' troubles by seizing some northern Thessalian towns. Alarmed at the prospect of a destructive war, some of Thessaly's clan chiefs asked Thebes, now Greece's leading power, to intervene. The Thebans responded immediately. They sent the stalwart Pelopidas north at the head of an army. Pelopidas kept the peace by creating a buffer zone guarded by his troops, on the northern Thessalian frontier. He also made a treaty with the Macedonian Alexander II in 368. However, a new round of diplomacy became necessary less than a year later when a local noble, Ptolemy of Alorus, murdered Alexander and became regent for the new king, Philip's other brother Perdiccas III.

To ensure that the unstable and apparently untrustworthy Macedonian royals would live up to their promises to keep the peace, upon returning to Thebes in 368, Pelopidas took with him a number of hostages. This act would indirectly have serious consequences for the Greek world. "He took Philip, the king's brother," Plutarch wrote, "and thirty other sons of the leading men of the state and brought them to Thebes as hostages. He did this to show the Greeks how far the prestige of Thebes had advanced."[7] Pelopidas had no way of knowing that the thirteen-year-old prince in his charge would one day come to intimidate and master the Thebans and other Greeks. During his three-year captivity in Thebes, this alert, shrewd, and farsighted boy would appraise his enemies' weaknesses and learn from their strengths. All the while he would patiently bide his time, confident that one day *he* would be master of Greece.

Chapter 3

An Overlord Among Equals

The teenage Philip of Macedonia remained in Thebes from 367 to 365 B.C. Although technically a prisoner, he was treated with the attention, kindness, and respect befitting his rank as an *aristocrat* (a term derived from the Greek word *aristoi*, meaning "best people"). The evidence for this was his stay as a guest in the home of Pammenes, one of the city's leading citizens, a choice of lodging for the boy that was to have fateful consequences. Pammenes was not only one of Thebes' most skilled generals, but also a close friend of Epaminondas, the victor of Leuctra and, at the time, the best military strategist of all Greece. From Epaminondas, Philip may have learned how the Theban troops trained and drilled, how infantry and cavalry could work together effectively, and how a supreme commander and his staff planned campaigns, strategies, and tactics. The boy certainly must have witnessed the magnificent Sacred Band training and drilling. Perhaps he even sensed then that some day this elite corps would prove his ultimate test. He could never hope to hold sway over Greece until he had faced and defeated these men on the battlefield.

Philip learned a great deal in his brief stay in Thebes. He saw firsthand the weaknesses of a democratic city-state. Political parties bickered among themselves, impeding progress. Also, through regular elections, top state administrators were frequently replaced, weakening executive power and making long-term planning difficult. And the government relied on a part-time citizen militia for the bulk of its army, with the result that, despite Epaminondas's diligent efforts, most soldiers lacked practical experience. Philip would later effectively exploit these weaknesses in his dealings with the classical poleis, both on and off the battlefield.

Philip's chance to begin applying some of the lessons he had learned in Thebes came earlier than he expected. Late in 365, his brother Perdiccas executed the royal regent, Ptolemy, and took full control of the Macedonian state. Almost immediately, Perdiccas arranged for Philip's return to Macedonia. He gave the younger man the huge task of training the kingdom's small, ragtag army into an effective fighting force. Philip had just begun to achieve positive results when, in 359, Perdiccas and some four thousand of his soldiers were killed while fighting the Illyrians. This group of tribal peoples, even more backward and uncultured than the

Despite efforts to improve military capabilities, Greek soldiers in citizen militias lacked experience. Philip would later use that inexperience to his advantage in conquering the Greek city-states.

Macedonians, occupied the mountainous region bordering Macedonia in the northwest (modern-day Albania) and periodically raided neighboring lands. Philip's chance had come. He assumed the Macedonian throne at the age of twenty-one or twenty-two.

A Land Long Divided

The situation facing Macedonia's young new ruler was daunting to say the least. First, though Philip was the last surviving son of Amyntus III and, therefore, next in line in the royal succession, some Macedonian nobles refused to recognize his claim to the throne. Various pretenders challenged him. Some were backed by foreign powers, such as Athens and Thrace, which created political chaos. Making matters worse, in the wake of Perdiccas's disastrous defeat, the country was militarily weaker than ever. Sensing easy victory, the Illyrians and the Paeonians, warlike tribesmen from north of Macedonia, got ready to invade. There seemed little hope that either the young, inexperienced Philip or the Macedonian state could survive. After all, most southern Greeks accurately saw Macedonia as a weak, corrupt cultural backwater with equally weak and corrupt leaders. "They regarded Macedonians in general as semi-savages," historian Peter Green pointed out, "uncouth of speech and dialect, retrograde in their political institutions, negligible as fighters, and habitual oath-breakers, who dressed in bear-pelts and were much given to . . . [drunkenness], tempered with regular bouts of assassination and incest."[1]

An examination of Macedonia before Philip's reign reveals the reasons for this sorry state of affairs. Since ancient times, Macedonia had been divided into two geographical, cultural, and political regions. The first was the lowlands, the fertile plain bordering the Aegean's Thermaic Gulf. This was the heart of the kingdom established by local cattle barons who had built their capital at Aegae, about thirty miles

During the summer of 1998, workers carefully sift through the dirt, searching for ancient artifacts in an ongoing archaeological dig in the Greek village of Vergina, site of the original Macedonian capital of Aegae.

west of the gulf. The second region was the highlands, a horseshoe-shaped plateau that encircled much of the lowland plain. In the rustic and independent highland strongholds, landholding tribal chiefs enforced their will on local peasants. The lowlanders and highlanders were almost constantly at odds, first one and then the other claiming authority over all of Macedonia. Not surprisingly, continuous disunity, political intrigues, and bloodletting impeded progress and kept the country from moving into the mainstream of Greek Aegean culture.

Eventually, however, some of Macedonia's lowland kings recognized that becoming part of that mainstream would enrich and empower them, perhaps enough to gain undisputed mastery over the highlands. To prove their "Greekness," Macedonian monarchs began to perpetuate stories linking their ancestry to prominent families in the southern poleis. In the early fifth century B.C., Alexander I—Philip's great-great-grandfather—made a show of competing in the Olympic Games, long seen as a Greek-only event. In a blatant effort to import Greek culture, Alexander's grandson Archelaus (who reigned 413–399) enthusiastically invited artists and intellectuals from Athens and other major city-states to spend time at the Macedonian court. Among these famous visitors were the painter Zeuxis and the dramatist Euripides, who wrote a play in Archelaus's honor.

Source Document

[It was] recognized by the managers of the Olympic games, on the occasion [in the early 400s B.C.] when Alexander [I] wished to compete and his Greek competitors tried to exclude him on the ground that foreigners were not allowed to take part. Alexander, however, proved his Argive descent, and so was accepted as a Greek and allowed to enter for the foot-race. . . . This Alexander was descended . . . from Perdiccas [I], who won the lordship of the Macedonians in the following way. Three brothers, Gauanes, Aeropus, and Perdiccas, descendants of Temenus, had been expelled from Argos . . . and crossed into upper Macedonia and . . . settled near the place called the Gardens of Midas, where roses grow wild. . . . It was from the slopes of these mountains that the brothers conquered, first, the land in the immediate neighbourhood, and afterwards the rest of Macedonia.[2]

Eager to prove to the city-states that they, too, were of Greek stock, the early Macdedonian monarchs claimed a link with Argos, a polis in the northeastern Peloponnesus, and descent from Temenus, a kinsman of the legendary Greek demigod Heracles. The fifth-century B.C. Greek historian Herodotus mentioned this claim in his Histories.

An Opportunity to Enter the Greek Mainstream

Archelaus's pro-Greek policies were also designed to expand Macedonia's economy by improving its political and trade relations with the important city-states. For a long time, the big powers of southern Greece had seen the Macedonian plains and hills as natural resources waiting to be exploited. In particular, poleis with huge military and merchant fleets, like Athens and Corinth, wanted the excellent shipbuilding lumber produced by Macedonia's abundant forests, a resource that had already been largely depleted in southern Greece. To this end, during the height of its empire Athens forced its way into the area. In 437 B.C., it founded the city of Amphipolis near the eastern side of Chalcidice, the three-fingered peninsula that forms the eastern rim of the Thermaic Gulf. Three years later, the Athenians seized control of Methone, on the Macedonian shore of the gulf. Through these outposts, Athens put military pressure on Macedonia, manipulated its timber exports, and interfered in its foreign policy.

By Archelaus's time, however, Athens was in dire straits due to the ravages of the Peloponnesian War. It had become more open to friendly negotiation. Archelaus saw improved relations with Athens as an opportunity to expand trade, strengthen his country, and enter the Greek cultural mainstream. To help the process along, sometime after 410, he moved the capital from Aegae to Pella, several miles to the

In the late fifth century B.C., *the Macedonian monarchy moved its capital from Aegae to Pella. Aegae remained the site of royal burials. This modern sign marks the entrance to the Macedonian tombs at Vergina.*

northeast. Pella had access to the gulf and the Aegean Sea. The old capital at Aegae remained the traditional burial site of Macedonian royalty.

But Archelaus's grand dreams soon evaporated. In 404, Athens went down in defeat. Less than five years later, the enlightened Macedonian king was assassinated and as royal pretenders rose and fell, highland chiefs warred for power. The Illyrians and other hostile tribes pressed in on the western and northern borders. Macedonia fell into a long generation of political anarchy and near ruin. Only Amyntus, Philip's father, was able to maintain some order in Pella and the lowlands. Through his reign and those of his first two sons, Alexander II and Perdiccas III, the Macedonian royal house survived only through tenacity and luck. This shaky kingship in a battered country was Philip's seemingly worthless inheritance as he took the throne in 359.

Philip's First Major Battle

Philip was confident that he could change the worthless into the worthwhile. Wise beyond his years and loaded with talent, energy, and determination, he immediately set about the first necessary order of business—unifying the country. To do this, he needed to assert strong authority over the Macedonian hill chiefs, who were still fiercely resentful of outside control. Even before tackling this objective, however, he needed to ward off the foreign tribes threatening the borders long enough for him to gain power. The young king realized his disadvantage. He temporarily held off the would-be invaders by paying them tribute, or money and other valuables. As for the Illyrians, he further cemented the deal by marrying Audata, an Illyrian princess.

Philip's submissive posture was a clever way to buy time, of course. Using ideas he may have learned from the Theban generals, he spent the winter of 359–358 B.C. rigorously training and drilling the small corps of troops he was able to gather from the lowland clans. In the spring, he marched north. He surprised the Paeonians, defeating them in a small battle and forcing them to recognize his authority. Wasting no time, he then turned southwest and attacked the far stronger Illyrians, led by his father-in-law, Bardylis. Here, in the first major battle of his career, Philip deftly applied the tactics Epaminondas had pioneered. Historian Peter Green described how Philip applied these tactics in this crucial early battle:

> Philip himself led the infantry, holding back his centre and left, deploying his line in the oblique echelon that was Epaminondas' specialty. As he had anticipated, the Illyrian right wing stretched and slewed [twisted] round to force an engagement. Philip waited until the inevitable, fatal gap appeared [in the enemy's line], and then sent in his right-wing cavalry, flank and rear. They drove a great wedge through the gap, and the Macedonian phalanx followed in their wake. A long and desperate struggle ensued. But at last . . . 7,000 Illyrians—three-quarters of Bardylis' entire force— were slaughtered.[3]

The National Army

With the border frontiers safe for the moment, Philip tackled the problem of gaining the allegiance of the Macedonian highlanders. He accomplished the task in a number of shrewd ways. The first and most important was a massive escalation of his military reform program. In contrast to the temporary militia used by the city-states, he began to create a national standing army. This was a completely new concept in warfare. His idea was to train a large permanent force of soldiers with tactics and discipline superior to the best mercenaries. He would pay them handsome rewards, composed both of generous land grants and the spoils gained in their victories. All the while, he would inspire them with a patriotic national spirit. Drawn by these powerful incentives, an increasing number of young men from all corners of Macedonia willingly gave their loyalty to Philip's national organization. The promise of lands and money, "along with the common training, the discipline and the service," commented classical historian J. R. Ellis,

> served to bind the army together as a unit with its allegiance to the king-commander, a tie that can only have been further strengthened by the lengthening string of victories won by it. The Macedonian state was historically heterogeneous [composed of dissimilar parts]; but the creation of a national army imbued with national goals and ideals provided a powerful impulse towards unity.[4]

Philip's new military system consisted of several different elements. Each complemented and strengthened the others. First, he introduced training and discipline far more rigorous than any before seen in Macedonia. According to Diodorus, for example, he made his men march up to thirty-five miles a day, carrying their weapons and wearing heavy packs. Philip also expanded the role and prestige of the *hetairoi*, or King's Companions, the elite cavalry corps of young noblemen first organized by his ancestor Alexander I. Long used mainly for skirmishing or guarding the king, the cavalry became a primary striking force trained to make frontal assaults on enemy armies.

In addition, Philip completely revolutionized the traditional Greek phalanx. First he deepened its ranks, as Epaminondas had done. Then he greatly increased the length of the soldiers' spears. Thousands of these *sarissas*, pikes ranging from twelve to perhaps eighteen feet or longer, projected from the front of the formation, giving it the look of a giant porcupine with its quills erect. When the Macedonian phalanx moved forward, this mass of men and metal was nearly unstoppable. Yet Philip did not design this formidable array as the supreme weapon in his arsenal. The secret of his success, and later that of Alexander, lay in their effective merging of different offensive elements— including the phalanx, cavalry, archers, peltasts, and new siege tactics—into a completely new unified, balanced, and coordinated arms system.

As this military system began to prove itself, and as Philip's reputation as a winning general grew, many Macedonian highlanders either gravitated to his ranks or saw that it was useless to oppose him, both of which had a national unifying effect. Philip also used more overt means to win. When a powerful lord resisted, for example, he was known to round up entire villages of the lord's local supporters and transplant them to distant regions of the country. This made the resisting lord powerless. To gain the cooperation of other highland nobles, Philip took their sons as hostages (a method he had learned from personal experience).

By these and other means, Philip rapidly accomplished what had for so long seemed a hopeless task—unifying upper and lower Macedonia into a powerful nation. His famous son would one day recall the scope and importance of this achievement while scolding some of his own soldiers. In a speech preserved by the Greek historian Arrian, Alexander said:

> Philip found you a tribe of impoverished vagabonds, most of you dressed in skins, feeding a few sheep on the hills and fighting, feebly enough, to keep them from your neighbors. . . . He gave you cloaks to wear instead of skins; he brought you down from the hills into the plains; he taught you to fight on equal terms with the enemy on your borders, till you knew that your safety lay not, as once, in your mountain strongholds, but in your own valor. He made you city-dwellers; he brought you the law; he civilized you.[5]

Europe's First National Power

Once Philip had gained either the support of or at least firm control over the highland nobles, he took care not to offend them. To put on kingly airs around these simple, rustic personalities, he realized, would only insult them. Thus, he made himself an overlord among equals. Unlike kings in foreign lands, he wore no royal robes or kingly insignia of any kind. Instead, he chose to dress, as he had in the past, like any other upper-class Macedonian. He rejected honorifics such as "sire" or "your majesty," allowing everyone to address him as Philip. In fact, he never described himself as a king in any official document.

Whatever titles he may have preferred, by 356 B.C., Philip, now twenty-six or twenty-seven, was the undisputed ruler of a vigorous and formidable new nation. In the words of noted historian David G. Hogarth, in less than four years Philip had created "the first European power in the modern sense . . . an armed nation with a common national ideal. This, his own conception, he understood clearly and pursued consistently through twenty-three years."[6] Philip had in mind a larger goal as well. He gazed south at the aging classical city-states, whose magnificent culture he so admired and wanted to imitate but whose wasteful disunity he despised. He saw clearly that the polis was an outmoded concept. Greece needed to become a single nation under a strong leader. He believed it was his destiny to be that leader.

Indeed, destiny was smiling on Philip and his house more than he knew at the time. In that same year, a son was born to him and his new wife, Olympias, a princess of Epirus, a small kingdom nestled between northwestern Greece and Illyria. On the day the boy, Alexander III, was born, the famous temple of the goddess Artemis at Ephesus in Ionia burned to the ground. Later, a joke circulated that it was no wonder the goddess's house was destroyed since she was so busy attending to Alexander's birth. Philip had just completed a successful siege of a town on the Chalcidian peninsula when he learned he had a son. He was elated, especially after local fortune-tellers assured him that the child would grow up to be invincible. Naturally enough, he wanted a strong heir who could carry on his national goals. Alexander may not have been invincible, but as the coming years would show, he was every inch his father's son.

Chapter 4

Warrior, Diplomat, and Schemer

Having pulled together the rival factions of Macedonia and secured his northern borders against the Paeonians and the Illyrians, Philip turned his attention to the south. He was fully aware that gaining control over all of Greece would be a monumental, if not impossible, task. Brimming with his usual energy and confidence, however, he felt up to the challenge. Whether his main objective was to conquer the Greeks or to unify them remains a point of debate among scholars. But even if conquest were his goal, destruction was not. The evidence suggests that he hoped to end petty bickering and fighting among the city-states and to lead them in more constructive enterprises. And there is little doubt that he looked forward to absorbing and defending, rather than destroying, their admirable arts and culture. As the noted classical historian J. B. Bury explained,

He was ambitious to secure a recognized hegemony in Greece . . . as had been held by Athens, by Sparta, and by Thebes in the days of their greatness; to form, in fact, a confederation of allies, which should hold some such dependent relation towards him. . . . Though the Greek states regarded Philip as . . . an outsider . . . it must never be forgotten that Philip desired to identify Macedonia with Greece, and to bring his own country up to the level of the kindred peoples who had so far outstripped it in civilisation. Throughout his whole career he regarded Athens with respect; he would have given much for her friendship and . . . deemed it one of his misfortunes that she compelled him to be her foe.[1]

To accomplish his goals, Philip realized, would likely involve war and bloodshed. For this he was prepared. But he preferred to use other means, especially diplomacy. He thought it stupid to waste good soldiers when there was an alternative to fighting. He also wanted to be remembered as Greece's champion, not its conqueror. And mostly he preferred diplomacy because he was proud of his brains and his ability to negotiate. According to Diodorus, Philip's success "was not due so much to his prowess in arms as to his adroitness and cordiality in diplomacy. Philip himself is said to have been prouder of his grasp of strategy and his diplomatic successes than of his valour in actual battle."[2] Philip's style of negotiation, however, often featured intrigue, half-truths, and outright double-dealing.

The Amphipolis Affair

Philip's skill as a warrior, diplomat, and schemer became apparent in his first major offensive against the city-states. He had set his sights on Amphipolis, which the Athenians had founded nearly eight decades before. Situated on the Strymon River in the frontier between Macedonia and Thrace, Amphipolis was a vital port for shipping Macedonian timber. The city was also the gateway to the rich gold mines of nearby Mount Pangaeus. Athens had lost the city, which became independent, a decade into the Peloponnesian War. Yet the Athenians still had close ties with the Amphipolitans.

Philip also considered seizing Pydna, an independent city located on the Thermaic Gulf. Pydna was friendly with Athens. By taking Pydna and Amphipolis, Philip might weaken Athenian influence in Macedonia's neighborhood. Late in 357 B.C., he laid siege to Amphipolis. The city "fell by storm," according to J. R. Ellis:

> After a series of assaults a section of the [city's defensive] wall was breached and the Macedonians pressed through the gap amidst fierce fighting, during which many defenders were killed, until the last resistance subsided. The victory, with siege-machinery playing a significant role in its achievement, marks the beginning of a long and successful Macedonian tradition [of expertise in siege warfare]; with the increasing sophistication of siege-equipment it became no longer exceptional that walled cities fell by direct assault.[3]

Upset over the city's fall, Athens declared war on Philip. But it was an empty gesture. At the time, the Athenians were preoccupied with troubles with some of their southern Aegean allies and could do nothing about Amphipolis. Moreover, they were surprised when soon after Philip seized the city, he generously reinstated its independence on the condition that it become his ally. Before the dazed Athenians had recovered from this surprise, he captured Pydna.

With Amphipolis and Pydna securely under his wing, Philip took the town of Crenides in the Mount Pangaeus mining area. He renamed it Philippi, after himself. The output of his subsequent mining operations brought him an immense annual income of over one thousand talents (Greek currency). This windfall provided Philip with plenty of cash for military expansion and, when the need arose, political bribery. In the meantime, by seizing the mining area, he had intruded into Thracian territory. So, over the next few years, he took the next logical step. He absorbed much of southern Thrace, provoking protests but no firm resistance from the region's tribal chiefs and king.

Philip Versus the Phocians

As Philip's increasingly powerful military machine ran largely unchecked through the northern Aegean, events in central and southern Greece began to play directly into his hands. In the mid-350s B.C., the small polis of Phocis, just south of Thessaly, suddenly rose to prominence. Under their ambitious leader Philomelus, the Phocians seized the religious sanctuary at Delphi, which rested within their territory. This started what became known as the Third Sacred War. The sanctuary, which all Greeks looked on as a common asset, housed the famous Delphic Oracle, a priestess (actually a succession of priestesses) who, people believed, acted as a medium between the gods and humans. Because religious pilgrims brought offerings of gold and other valuables, the local temples were also storehouses of tremendous wealth, which Philomelus and his followers now controlled.

Expecting opposition from other Greeks, Philomelus tried to gain the support of powerful city-states. Diodorus recorded how Philomelus

> sent envoys to the . . . most distinguished cities of the Greek world, explaining that he had seized Delphi, not with any designs upon its sacred properties but to assert a claim to the guardianship of the sanctuary . . . ordained in early times as belonging to the Phocians. He said he would render due account of the property to all the Greeks and . . . requested that . . . these cities should preferably join forces with him. . . .[4]

Sparta and several other states offered to back Phocis, but Thebes and some of its Boeotian allies declared war. After many months of fighting, the Phocians emerged stronger than ever, mainly because they used the money from the Delphic treasuries to hire large numbers of mercenaries. For a while, it looked as if Phocis might become one of Greece's major powers.

However, the overconfident Phocians made the mistake of meddling in the affairs of their neighbors, the Thessalians and Thessaly sent out a cry for help to its own neighbor, Macedonia. Philip—already looking for an excuse to make his move into southern Greece—was only too glad to oblige. The Phocians managed to hold their own against him for several months. But using his formidable new version of the phalanx, Philip

On his way south to fight the Phocians, Philip passed by Mount Olympus, thought to be home of the Greek gods, in northern Thessaly. This view of the central peaks is from the picturesque modern village of Litichoro.

defeated them. In 353, the remaining Phocians fled south. Philip then took charge of Thessaly, including its rich agricultural plain and large stocks of fine cavalry horses.

With the exception of the Chalcidian peninsula in the northwestern Aegean, Philip now controlled all of Greece north of the pass of Thermopylae, on Thessaly's southeast border, the strategic gateway to the southern city-states. Incredibly, though, these states still did not consider Philip a serious threat to their security. It is likely that their view of him remained distorted by their contempt for the weak and corrupt Macedonia of the past—a dangerous mistake in judgment, for which they would eventually pay dearly.

The Fall of Olynthus

Only one important public figure recognized and called attention to the threat Philip posed— Demosthenes of Athens, one of Greece's greatest orators. In 351 B.C., he delivered the first of his *Philippics*, speeches denouncing Philip's aggressions. "Observe, Athenians," Demosthenes declared,

> the height to which the fellow's insolence has soared: he leaves you no choice of action or inaction; he blusters and talks big . . . [and] he cannot rest content with what he has conquered; he is always taking in more, everywhere casting his net around us, while we sit idle and do nothing. When, Athenians, will you take the necessary action? What are you waiting for? Until you are compelled, I presume.[5]

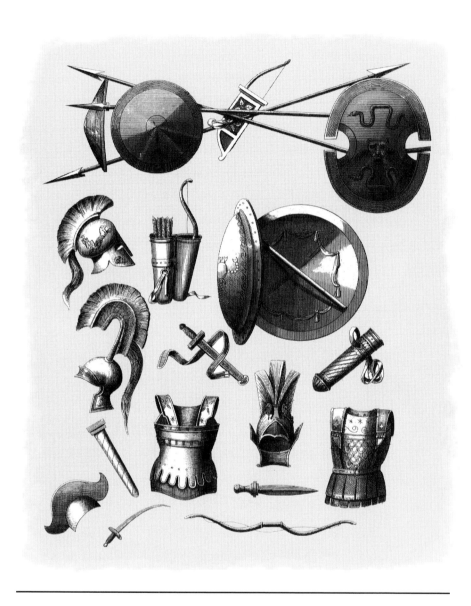

Weapons and armor used by the Greek infantry.

Demosthenes presumed correctly. Few Athenians or other Greeks heeded his words. Shortly after the delivery of Demosthenes's *First Philippic*, Philip made his next move. His target was Olynthus, a commercially successful polis in the western Chalcidice and the head of the Chalcidian league of cities. As fear swept through Chalcidice, the Olynthians, realizing they had no chance against Philip, desperately appealed to Athens for help. The feisty Demosthenes rose to the occasion. He delivered three magnificent speeches, later dubbed the *Olynthiacs*. He demanded that his countrymen aid their fellow Greeks against the "barbaric" interloper from the north. "In a word, he has hoodwinked everyone who has had any dealings with him," the orator raged:

> He has played upon the folly of each party in turn and exploited their ignorance of his own character. That is how he has gained his power. . . . What better time or occasion could you find than the present, men of Athens? When will you do your duty, if not now? Has not your enemy already captured all our strongholds, and if he becomes master of the Chalcidice, shall we not be overwhelmed with dishonor? . . . Is not Philip our enemy? And in possession of our property? And a barbarian? Is any description too bad for him? But, in the name of the gods, when we have abandoned all these places and almost helped Philip to gain them, shall we then ask who is to blame?[6]

Although Demosthenes managed to stir up some alarm among his fellow Athenians, they decided to send most of their available troops to quell local rebellions on Euboea, the large island lying along Attica's east coast. Eventually, in the autumn of 348, they sent two thousand mercenaries under a general named Chares to help the Olynthians. Philip probably would have easily brushed aside this pitifully inadequate force had it arrived in time. While it was on its way, Olynthus fell to the Macedonian king's mighty siege machines. As an example to other Chalcidians who might dare to defy him, he leveled the city and condemned most of its inhabitants to slavery.

The Athenians Are Dumbstruck

At this point, Athens, which was still not prepared to fight the Macedonians, decided that the best way to stop Philip's aggression was to make a deal with him. Ten Athenian ambassadors, including Demosthenes and Aeschines, another brilliant orator who often opposed Demosthenes's hawkish (warlike) policies, journeyed north and met with Philip. The negotiations produced an agreement. Macedonia promised not to interfere in the Thracian Chersonese, the peninsula bordering the Hellespont that protected the route to the Euxine Sea (now called the Black Sea). For generations, Athens had depended on grain grown in the fertile lands bordering the Euxine. In fact, it had been Sparta's capture of this grain route that had forced the Athenians' final surrender in the Peloponnesian War. In return for Philip's promise to keep his hands off the Chersonese, Athens pledged, undoubtedly with great reluctance, to give up its long-standing claim to Amphipolis.

But Philip soon surprised and angered the Athenians once again. In July 346 B.C., less than two years after he had made the agreement with the Athenians, the Macedonian king double-crossed them. Using the excuse of the Phocians' continued control of Delphi, Philip boldly moved part of his army through the pass of Thermopylae and into southern Greece. He swiftly overran Phocis and forced the Phocian garrison from the Delphic sanctuary. As the ancient biographer Plutarch described it, "The news stunned the Athenians. No speaker dared to mount the rostrum, nobody knew what advice should be given, the assembly was struck dumb and appeared to be completely at a loss."[7]

Indeed, the question of what the unpredictable Macedonian King Philip would do next was on everyone's lips. While all Greece held its breath, the old orator Isocrates stepped forward. For decades, he had been incessantly badgering Greek leaders about uniting against the Persians, but few had paid him any serious attention. The daring and powerful Philip now seemed the perfect person to make Isocrates's Panhellenic dream a reality. In the autumn of 346, Isocrates published his *Address to Philip*. In it, he emphasized that the Persians were cowards and poor fighters. He argued that a crusade against them would keep the thousands of landless and unemployed mercenaries who were now roaming Greece busy. And

Persia's vast wealth would better serve the inherently "superior" Greeks than the Persian "barbarians." "Consequently," the orator concluded,

> I am now addressing myself to you, although I am not unaware that when I am proposing this course many will look at it askance, but that when you are actually carrying it out all will rejoice in it; for . . . when the benefits from it shall have been realized in fact, everyone without fail will . . . look to have his portion.[8]

Philip was already quite familiar with Isocrates's ideas, of course. But he welcomed this fresh appeal from the old man for its obvious propaganda value. The Greeks of the city-states fully expected the Macedonian king, a proven political manipulator, to take advantage of this unexpected "good press." What they did not realize at the time was that Philip, a passionate devotee of Greek culture, had also taken Isocrates's idea to heart.

Chapter 5

To Decide the Fate of Greece

Shortly after he had forced the Phocians from Delphi, Philip sat unchallenged on the Amphyctionic Council, the elite, politically neutral religious body that administered the sanctuary. As an added reward for "liberating" the holy area, the council gave him Phocis' two traditional council seats. They also invited him to preside over that year's Pythian Games, Panhellenic athletic contests—second in importance only to those held at Olympia—that the council presented every four years to honor the god Apollo. For Philip, these rewards surely had an added, special dimension. After years of fighting to be accepted into Greece's political and cultural main-stream, here at least was some official recognition that he was a genuine Greek.

Yet some Greeks still refused to accept Philip as anything less than an uncultured barbarian and ruthless conqueror. Their collective voice found expression through Demosthenes, who now stridently warned that Philip would next invade Attica and try to subjugate Athens. It is hardly likely, however, that this was Philip's intention. Because Athens was the recognized center of the Greek arts and culture he so admired, he would want to keep the city intact. Also, he had no navy to speak of, whereas Athens had many ships, which, if necessary, could keep the city, barricaded as it was behind its Long Walls, supplied

Philip spared Athens partly because he deeply admired Athenian culture, as exemplified by this architectural masterpiece, the Porch of the Maidens on the south side of the Erechtheum temple on the Acropolis.

indefinitely. Attacking Athens and then failing to take it would only drain his resources and damage his reputation. It is more likely that Philip hoped for some kind of Macedonian-Athenian alliance, with himself at its head. And indeed, some pro-Panhellenic Athenian politicians advocated this very idea before the city's assembly.

But Demosthenes's anti-Macedonian voice and influence grew increasingly dominant in Athens. In 344 B.C., he delivered his *Second Philippic*, saying,

> One day Philip's policy will cause you more distress than it does now, for I see the plot thickening. I hope I may prove a false prophet, but I fear the catastrophe is even now only too near. So when you can no longer shut your eyes to what is happening . . . then I expect that you will be angry and exasperated.[1]

As more Athenians and other Greeks began listening to Demosthenes, his political power steadily increased. He persuaded the government to institute a program of naval expansion. He also secretly bribed leaders in other cities to come out against Philip. Not long after Demosthenes lashed out with his third mighty *Philippic* in 341, Philip resigned himself to the inevitability of war with the Athenians. It would be on a bloody battlefield in Boeotia that he would eventually face them and their allies to decide the fate of all Greece.

A Desire for Fame and Glory

Philip tried to put off the confrontation as long as he could. Though he had planted a strong foothold in southern Greece, as usual, he took the time to consolidate his gains and build new power and support everywhere he could. For instance, in the late 340s B.C., while Demosthenes was denouncing him from the rostrum, Philip pushed into central and northern Thrace. In hard-fought campaigns, he dethroned the Thracian king and made Thrace a province of Macedonia. This not only greatly expanded Philip's domain and resources but also extended Macedonia's frontiers to the border of the Thracian Chersonese. This put Philip in a position to strike at Athens' precious grain route at his will. Spurred on by Demosthenes, the Athenians sent ships and mercenaries to the Chersonese. These forces unwisely raided some of Philip's Thracian outposts, further increasing tensions between Macedonia and Athens.

Meanwhile, during these years, Philip's remarkably intelligent and energetic son, Alexander, had reached his early teens. Even at this young age, Alexander was apparently consumed by a desire to achieve great fame and glory. To this end, he was eager to join in his father's conquests of the Greek city-states. But Philip wisely insisted that the time was not yet right for Alexander to take part in military campaigns. Instead, Philip kept his ambitious teenage son busy absorbing Greek knowledge and culture. Alexander was fortunate to have had one of the greatest teachers who ever lived, which undoubtedly accounted in no small part for his later success as a leader. Plutarch wrote that Philip considered that the task of training and educating his son was too important to be entrusted to the ordinary run of teachers . . . so he sent for Aristotle, the most famous and learned of the philosophers of his time, and rewarded him with the generosity that his reputation deserved. . . . At first Alexander greatly admired Aristotle and became more attached to him than to his father, for the one, he used to say, had given him the gift of life, but the other had taught him how to live well.[2]

Though grateful to his father for having brought the great Aristotle to Pella to be his tutor, Alexander remained anxious to see military action. According to ancient sources, he became increasingly jealous of Philip's successes. "Whenever he heard that Philip had captured some famous city or won an overwhelming victory," commented Plutarch, "Alexander would show no pleasure at the news. . . . He believed that the more he received from his father, the less would be left for him to conquer."[3] Finally, when the boy was sixteen, Philip gave him a taste of the action. While away campaigning, the king left his son in charge of the country, allowing Alexander the title of regent. It was in this capacity that Alexander showed himself militarily and politically capable beyond his years by putting down an Illyrian rebellion, founding a new city, and receiving and greatly impressing envoys of the Persian king.

The City-States Prepare to Fight

After these successes, the ambitious Macedonian prince was eager for a stronger test. He soon got his

This statue of the renowned Greek philosopher-scientist Aristotle, whom Philip hired to tutor young Alexander, rests in a busy square in the northern Greek city of Thessaloniki, once part of the Macedonian heartland.

wish. Philip took Alexander along in 338 B.C. when the Macedonian Army marched toward its final confrontation with the southern city-states. In the preceding two years, in what must be considered Demosthenes's finest hour, the orator had almost single-handedly forged a powerful anti-Macedonian alliance. Having witnessed much of what he had predicted about Philip come true, many Greeks saw him as the patriotic leader of the moment. "All Greece seemed . . . up in arms to support Demosthenes for the future," Plutarch recalled, "so much so that not only did the Athenian generals take their orders from him, but also the Boeotarchs [Theban generals]."[4]

In fact, Demosthenes clearly recognized the essential need of winning over the Thebans to his cause. He had always had a fondness for Thebes and strongly believed that the Thebans still possessed the military prowess that had, two decades prior, vaulted them to their domination of Greece. Sparta, still resentful over its losses at Leuctra and Mantinea, refused to get involved. An alliance with Thebes now seemed the only realistic way for Athens to save itself and the rest of Greece. For their part, the Thebans had no great love or respect for the Athenians. The two peoples had been enemies more often than friends over the years. But Theban leaders reasoned correctly that to abandon Athens now might only lead to their own ruin: If Philip managed to defeat and absorb Greece's leading city, he would surely turn on Thebes, which would be left standing largely alone against him. Thus, in the spring of 338,

Thebes signed the pact Demosthenes had engineered and hastily prepared for the coming fight.

That summer, Philip and Alexander moved their army east from Phocis. The Athenian and Theban forces, along with small contingents from Corinth, Megara, and a few other neighboring poleis, converged to block their path. The allies set up their defensive line in the Cephisus Valley near Chaeronea in western Boeotia. They had chosen a strong position protected by mountains on all sides but the north. This left the Macedonians no choice but a frontal assault from that direction. Though the allied infantry was superior in numbers—possessing perhaps thirty-five thousand hoplites compared with the enemy's thirty thousand—the opposing cavalry units were evenly matched at about two thousand each.

Philip was no doubt unimpressed by either the enemy's strong position or the sheer number of allied troops. He was confident that his superbly trained, battle-hardened veterans were more than a match for the mostly unseasoned militiamen in the opposing army except, of course, for the Theban Sacred Band. Philip knew that he had to destroy this crack regiment at all costs. After that, he hoped, the rest of the allies would crumble. Sometime in late July or early August, Philip grimly but calmly marched his forces south into the Cephisus Valley toward what he must have seen as his great date with destiny.

Disaster at Chaeronea

On the morning of August 4, 338 B.C., the armies of Macedonia and the allied city-states arrayed themselves on the field in preparation for what would prove one of the more decisive battles in Western history. Peter Green described the breakdown of the opposing forces:

> On the allied right wing were the Boeotians, some 12,000 strong, led by the . . . Sacred Band. . . . On the left wing were stationed Athens' 10,000 hoplites. The centre was made up from the remaining allied contingents, with a stiffening of 5,000 mercenaries. . . . The cavalry was held in reserve. The Greek commanders had drawn up their line of battle slantwise across the plain, from west-south-west to east-north-east. . . . [Philip's] tactical dispositions were made accordingly. He himself commanded the right wing . . . [and] in the centre he placed the regiments of the phalanx. The command of the heavy cavalry on the extreme left wing, opposite the Sacred Band, went to Alexander—an extraordinarily responsible appointment for a boy of eighteen, since it was he who had to deliver the knock-out blow.[5]

The battle began as Philip's forces, marshalled in their now customary oblique formation, advanced on the stationary allies. The Macedonian right wing clashed with some of the Athenians on the allied far left. The rest of Philip's line kept itself angled farther back, giving the impression that it was reluctant to engage the enemy. The overconfident Athenian generals took the bait. They led a spirited charge, one of them shouting, "Come on, let's drive them back to

Macedonia!"[6] On and on came the Athenian hoplites, Demosthenes himself lumbering along in their enthusiastic ranks. All the while, the Macedonian infantrymen, with their thousands of forward-pointing *sarissas* forming an impenetrable metal wall, slowly and coolly continued to back away. This caused the troops of the allied left and center to drift increasingly to the left and away from their allies, the Thebans, who had maintained their original position more than half a mile away on the far right.

Eventually, as Philip had brilliantly anticipated, a fatal gap opened in the allied lines. Responding immediately, Alexander led his cavalry against the now isolated Thebans. He quickly surrounded them. At the same time, Philip suddenly ordered his lethal phalanx forward, halting the charge of the surprised Athenians and other allies, who now began to fall back in disorder. The Macedonian pikemen began to mow down everyone in their path. It was not long before the allies, including most of the Thebans, were in full retreat. Even the tough-talking Demosthenes ran for his life. "So far from achieving anything honorable," wrote Plutarch, "he completely failed to suit his actions to his words. He . . . took to his heels in the most shameful fashion, throwing away his arms in order to run faster."[7]

Of the whole allied army, only the members of the Sacred Band resolutely stood their ground, preferring death to dishonor. Already damaged by Alexander's devastating cavalry attack, they now faced part of

Source Document

The Sacred band . . . consisted of three hundred picked men, who were given their training and lodging by the city and were quartered on the Cadmea [the central fortress]. . . . According to some accounts, this force was composed of lovers and beloved. . . . Tribesmen or clansmen do not feel any great concern for their kinfolk in time of danger, but a band which is united by the ties of love is truly indissoluble and unbreakable, since both lovers and beloved are ashamed to be disgraced in the presence of the other, and each stands his ground at a moment of danger to protect the other. . . . It was natural, therefore, that the Band was termed Sacred for the same reason that Plato describes the lover as a friend "inspired by God," and it [the band] . . . was never defeated until the battle of Chaeronea. The story goes that when King Philip of Macedon was inspecting the dead after the fighting, he stood at the place where the three hundred had faced the long pikes of his phalanx, and lay dead in their armor, their bodies piled one upon the other. He was amazed at the sight, and when he learned that this was the band of lovers and beloved, he wept and exclaimed, "A curse on those who imagine that these men ever did or suffered anything shameful!"[8]

In his biography of the Theban statesman Pelopidas, the first-century A.D. Greek biographer Plutarch included this description of Thebes' famous Sacred Band, the group's uncommon valor, and the tribute Philip paid it after it had been annihilated at Chaeronea.

Philip's phalanx, which had wheeled around behind them. Still, they valiantly refused to retreat. There they died, and with them that day perished the last hope of the traditional city-states. As domination over Greece had once passed from Athens to Sparta and then to Thebes, it now passed to Macedonia, which cared nothing for the old ideal of the independent polis.

When the news of the disaster at Chaeronea reached Athens a few hours later, fear gripped the city. While Athenian leaders handed out weapons to noncitizens, even slaves, the naval arsenals at Piraeus desperately began preparing for a siege. This reaction proved unwarranted, however. In fact, Philip is said to have been distressed at learning that the Athenians expected him to lay waste to their city. As everyone would soon learn, he had far more constructive plans for Athens and for Greece.

Chapter 6

A Vision of the Future

After his victory at Chaeronea, Philip treated Thebes harshly, perhaps feeling it prudent to humble and weaken what had so recently been Greece's major land power. He began by executing or confiscating the lands of Thebes' anti-Macedonian leaders. He also installed a military garrison on the Cadmea, just as Sparta had done years before. Then he severely reduced the city-state's power by breaking up the Boeotian league, from which Thebes drew essential manpower and material support.

The Athenians, by contrast, were surprised and relieved when their enemy treated them much more mercifully. Philip offered to return unharmed the two thousand Athenians he had captured at Chaeronea and promised not to march his troops into Attica. In return, he demanded that Athens surrender the

Thracian Chersonese to him and willingly follow him as head of a Hellenic confederacy that he proposed to create. The Athenians realized that they were getting off easy. They immediately accepted his terms. Even Demosthenes grudgingly admitted that Philip's offer was generous.

Of course, Philip had good reasons for dealing leniently with Athens. One of them was his genuine love and respect for the city's high culture. Perhaps even more important, however, he respected Athens' formidable navy. Consisting of well over three hundred ships, the navy was still intact. It could prove a difficult and dangerous obstacle if he chose to invade Attica. Besides, Philip probably realized that he would desperately need these ships later to transport troops and supplies across the Aegean Sea to Asia Minor. Perhaps inspired in part by Isocrates's Panhellenic dreams, Philip was intent on leading a united Greek alliance in a grand conquest of the Asian "barbarians."

In this regard, Philip's political genius had led him to a vision of the future more advanced and realistic than the old separatist ideals to which the city-states still clung. After savaging one another for centuries, he reasoned, the poleis needed a savior, a single strong leader who would both unite and protect them. But for the prosperity and peace of mind this unity and protection would bring them, they would have to give up something they held dear—their independence. As classical historian George Cawkwell put it, Macedonia was a national state far richer and far more populous than any Greek city-state. When Philip realized its potential, it was inevitable that the world of the independent city-state would pass away. . . . They had to unite either against him or under him. Independence as they had known it was no longer possible.[1]

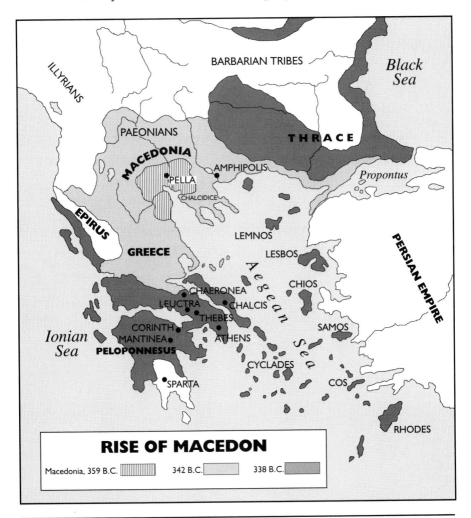

Philip of Macedonia succeeded in uniting enormous parts of Greece under his rule.

A Desire to Avoid Further Bloodshed

The proof of Philip's constructive plans for those he
had vanquished lay not only in his lenient treatment of
Athens but also in his policy toward southern Greece
as a whole. It came as a surprise to many when he did
not attempt to incorporate into Macedonia any of the
city-states stretching from Thessaly south. Earlier,
Thrace had been made a Macedonian province, and
the lands of conquered northern cities such as
Methone and Olynthus had been divided and parceled
out to Macedonian landowners. Thus, Philip had
ruthlessly expanded his kingdom's borders at the
expense of his immediate northern neighbors. But he
stopped short of absorbing the southern poleis, partly
out of respect for their high culture but also because in
the long run he wanted their willing cooperation
rather than their resentful subservience. After
Chaeronea, M. B. Sakellariou wrote, Philip seemed

> determined to avoid any unnecessary shedding of
> Greek blood or waste of Greek wealth, and to do
> nothing that might make him appear to be a
> conqueror. Rather than to domineer, Philip tried to
> gain the ascendancy in southern Greece with the
> consent, or at least the toleration, of the majority of
> the Greeks and to run counter to their wishes as little
> as he could.[2]

The most conspicuous example of Philip's attempt
to avoid further bloodshed was the way he dealt with
the problem of Sparta. Not long after Chaeronea, he
entered the Peloponnesus. The Peloponnesian states

had so far remained neutral. As he marched southward, Corinth, Argos, and the others wisely submitted to him without a fight. Only the Spartans stood their ground and refused to acknowledge his authority. They would not even meet with him. When he wrote asking whether he should come as friend or foe, they boldly replied, "Neither."

As everyone knew, Sparta's glory days were over. It had no real chance against Philip. Yet Sparta's tiny army might still inflict serious damage. Philip had to consider the strong possibility that if he attacked, every Spartan might fight to the death, forcing him to exercise the harsh measures he wanted to avoid. Therefore, Philip chose not to invade Sparta. Instead, he seized its outlying frontiers and divided these lands among his allies. In this way, Philip neutralized the Spartans by isolating them within a ring of states he controlled.

The Hellenic League

Having secured the Peloponnesus, Philip began the task of creating a true Panhellenic alliance. In September 338 B.C., he invited (*ordered* would be more accurate) all the Greek mainland states and many of the island poleis to attend a grand assembly, over which he would preside. With the exception of Sparta, everyone obeyed. Philip's choice of Corinth for the meeting was intended to have symbolic meaning in two ways. First, the Isthmus of Corinth lay roughly in the center of southern Greece. Second, and more important, during the Persian onslaught in 480, the Greek allies had met at Corinth to plan their resistance against the invaders. Philip wanted to send the message that the time for a new alliance had now arrived.

Philip carefully refrained from discussing Persia at the opening session of the congress, sometime late in 338. Instead, the delegates considered the structure of the confederation itself, the obligations of member states, and the roles Macedonia and its king would play. Philip had already drafted his version of the alliance. Everyone was expected to accept it with little or no alteration. Peter Green summed up the main points:

> The Greek states were to make a common peace . . . with one another, and constitute themselves into a federal Hellenic League. This league would take joint decisions by means of a federal council . . . on which each state would be represented according to its size and military importance. . . . Simultaneously, the league was to form a separate alliance with Macedonia, though Macedonia itself would not be a member. This treaty was to be made with "Philip and his descendants" in perpetuity. The king would act as "leader" (hegemon) of the league's joint forces, a combined civil and military post designed to provide for the general security of Greece. . . . If the Greeks were involved in a war, they could call on Macedonia to support them. Equally, if Philip needed military aid, he was entitled to requisition contingents from the league.[3]

However, no matter how much Philip tried to disguise it, the fact that he would be making all the decisions was plain. Three of the thirteen obligations the delegates had to accept clearly spelled out his unlimited authority. The seventh obligation compelled league members to carry out all of the hegemon's orders without question. The twelfth forbade anyone to commit hostile acts against Philip or his heirs. And the thirteenth forced all states to join in punishing any member that violated the agreement.

Although most of Philip's motives were self-promoting and exploitative, he had given the Greeks unity at last. As historian N.G.L. Hammond stated,

> What Philip created was "the community of the Greeks." Within a year the Greek Community developed an agreed system of administration, which was far in advance of the present system of the European Community. The number of each state's members and so votes on the Council was decided on a form of proportional representation which was related to military and naval strengths. The decisions of the Council by majority vote were binding on both the Council and on the member-states. . . . It was a self-standing state, which banned internal wars among its members and revolutionary party-strife within each member, and which insisted on the maintenance of peace and the rule of law. . . . Philip showed remarkable foresight. He realized that the desire for peace and independence was very strong, and that if the city-states of the [Greek] mainland and the Aegean islands should remain at peace they would develop greater prosperity.[4]

Despite its potential advantages, few Greeks were pleased with the new arrangement. This was partly because their rivalries and hatreds ran deep. They did not look forward to having to get along. They also still saw Philip as a barbaric outsider and resented that he was imposing his will on them by conquest. Yet some had to admit that he had professed a willingness to negotiate long before Chaeronea and that the Greeks, to some degree, may have brought his military solution upon themselves. The peace they were now forced to accept, historian Eugene N. Borza pointed out, "was not unlike what Philip had first offered the Greeks through diplomacy beginning nearly a decade before. This fact remains the most important single argument favoring the sincerity of those earlier proposals."[5]

Philip's Untimely Demise

Whatever the feelings harbored by the alliance's members, all now found themselves irresistibly swept along in the tide of Philip's grandiose plans for the conquest of Persia. He officially announced his intentions (which were already common knowledge) at the Congress of Corinth's second meeting in 337 B.C., calling for a crusade to punish the Persians for their "sacrilegious" invasion of Greece more than a century before. This excuse for the expedition was nothing more than window dressing, of course, and everyone knew it. But once again, having no real choice, the member states complied. They unanimously chose Philip as the expedition's supreme commander and

Source Document

Before long the domestic strife that resulted from Philip's various marriages and love-affairs . . . led to bitter clashes and accusations between father and son. This breach was widened by Olympias, a woman of jealous and vindictive temper, who incited Alexander to oppose his father. Their quarrel was brought to a head on the occasion of the wedding of [Philip and] Cleopatra. . . . Cleopatra's uncle Attalus, who had drunk too much at the banquet, called upon the Macedonians to pray to the gods that the union of Philip and Cleopatra might bring forth a legitimate heir to the throne. Alexander flew into a rage at these words, shouted at him, "Villain, do you take me for a bastard, then?" and hurled a drinking-cup at his head. At this Philip lurched to his feet, and drew his sword against his son, but fortunately for them both he was so overcome with drink and with rage that he tripped and fell headlong. Alexander jeered at him and cried out, "Here is the man who was making ready to cross from Europe to Asia, and who cannot even cross from one table to another without losing his balance."[6]

One of the most famous stories about Philip and Alexander suggests that, in the period following Philip's divorce of Alexander's mother, Olympias, the relationship between father and son, long colored by an element of rivalry simmering beneath the surface, became openly strained. Plutarch described their quarreling.

pledged the necessary soldiers, ships, and supplies. Wasting little time, the following spring, Philip sent an advance force under Generals Parmenio and Attalus to secure the area around the Hellespont and achieve a foothold in northwestern Asia Minor.

However, Philip himself was destined never to set foot on Persian soil. The chain of events leading to his untimely end may have begun in 337, when he divorced Olympias and married Cleopatra, the young niece of his trusted general, Attalus. Cleopatra was perhaps Philip's seventh wife and the first of Macedonian birth. All the others had been foreigners he had married to cement diplomatic alliances. Philip's marriage to Cleopatra was the first time he married for love. Both Olympias and her son, the impetuous Prince Alexander, were furious. The boy and his father had a serious falling-out at the wedding feast, and Alexander and Olympias may have begun plotting Philip's demise at this time. The birth the following year of Philip and Cleopatra's son, who represented a possible threat to Alexander's succession as king, made the scheme, if indeed there was one, seem all the more justified. Although conclusive evidence is lacking, some scholars think it likely that mother and son egged on the actual assassin, a disgruntled Macedonian named Pausanias, who had already been poorly treated by Philip and held a grudge.

The fatal blow came at another wedding celebration, this one in honor of the union between Philip's daughter (also named Cleopatra) and a prince of Epirus. As Diodorus recounted, the theater in which the party took place was full:

> Philip appeared wearing a white cloak, and by his express orders his bodyguard held away from him and followed only at a distance, since he wanted to show publicly that he was protected by the goodwill of all the Greeks, and had no need of a guard. . . . When [Pausanias] saw that the king was left alone, [he] rushed at him, pierced him [with a dagger] through his ribs, and stretched him out dead; then ran for the . . . horses which he had prepared for his flight.[7]

The remains of the small theater adjoining the Macedonian palace at Aegae. When Philip stepped out, alone, into the theater's central area, an assassin leapt from the crowd and stabbed him to death.

These column bases at the palace at Vergina (Aegae) mark the site of the wedding celebration Philip and Alexander attended immediately before Philip's assassination.

But the assassin did not get far. Several young aristocrats caught up with him and killed him with their spears. All of these avengers were Alexander's close friends, lending credence to the idea that they had been instructed beforehand to silence Pausanias before he could reveal his accomplices' identities.

Most of Greece was overjoyed at Philip's death. When the news reached Athens, for instance, people celebrated openly and gave thanks with sacrifices to the gods. Plutarch later criticized this behavior:

> For my part I cannot say that the Athenians did themselves any credit . . . to celebrate the death of a king who, when he was the conqueror and they the conquered, had treated them with such tolerance and humanity. . . . It was a contemptible action to . . . pay [Philip] honors while he was alive, and then, as soon as he had fallen by another's hand, to be beside themselves with joy, trample on his body, and sing paeans [hymns] of victory.[8]

Whether it was justified or honorable, the Athenians' celebration was decidedly premature. They likely assumed that, at the tender age of twenty, Alexander lacked the strength, skill, and experience needed to replace his father and hold together the Hellenic alliance. However, the Athenians, like their fellow Greeks, would soon learn that, for them, nothing had really changed except the name of the Macedonian king.

Chapter 7

The Inheritors of a Vision

Though Alexander was as brilliant and ambitious as his father, the two had very different personalities and goals. As a general and politician, Philip was patient and methodical, content with setting long-term objectives and then taking as many years as necessary to fulfill them. By contrast, Alexander was both impetuous and impatient. According to some ancient sources, he believed that, like several of the heroes in Greek legends, he was destined to die young. Therefore, he would have to squeeze a lifetime's worth of achievements into a short span. Philip, an extrovert in his private life, enjoyed getting drunk and carousing with women. In this regard, Alexander was much more restrained. According to Plutarch, "In spite of his vehement and impulsive nature, he showed

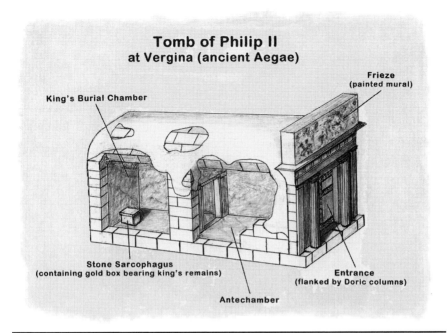

Tomb of Philip II
at Vergina (ancient Aegae)

A cutaway view of the tomb widely believed to be Philip's. The tomb is now part of a magnificent museum enclosing most of the Macedonian royal cemetery.

little interest in the pleasures of the senses and indulged in them only with great moderation."[1]

In particular, though both men earnestly sought glory, they differed on its meaning and rewards. For Philip, the conquest of Asia was a practical move, designed to enrich and empower Macedonia. It also provided a common enemy for the Greek states in his Hellenic League. As long as they were fighting someone else, he reasoned, they were less likely to squabble with him or among themselves. But the idealistic Alexander viewed the Asiatic campaign more as a divinely inspired crusade that he was destined to lead and that would secure him everlasting fame. In fact, he apparently thought that he was himself part god and that this gave him the natural right to conquer and rule over other human beings. Aristotle had taught him the importance of attaining *arete*, roughly translated as personal excellence in all things. The pursuit of this ideal guided all of the young man's future actions. "Those who endure hardship and danger," Alexander later declared, "are the ones who achieve glory; and the most gratifying thing is to live with courage and to die leaving behind eternal renown."[2]

No Mere Boy

After ascending the Macedonian throne and taking charge of his father's army in 336 B.C., Alexander at once demonstrated his remarkable energy, strength, and determination. He raced south to serve notice on the southern city-states that he was no mere boy to be trifled with. Greek leaders were stunned by his swift appearance and commanding authority. Without striking a blow, he reaffirmed Macedonia's control of the Hellenic League. Then he hurried back home, having learned that many of the tribes on the frontiers of Macedonia—also hoping to take advantage of his youth and inexperience—had rebelled. In a lightning campaign, Alexander easily crushed these insurgents.

In 335, while Alexander was concluding his operations in the north, a false rumor of his death quickly spread through Greece. Once more, highly premature celebrations erupted everywhere. Thebes made the mistake of launching a full-scale revolt. The Theban rebels stormed the Macedonian garrison on the Cadmea, but the besieged men managed to hold out for the short time it took Alexander to dash south again to their aid. The young king dealt much more harshly with Thebes than his father had. Alexander ordered every building in the city destroyed, with the exception of the temples (lest he be accused of sacrilege) and the house of the poet Pindar, whose writings he greatly admired. At least six thousand Thebans were killed. Another thirty thousand, mostly women and children, were sold into slavery. These cold-blooded acts discouraged would-be rebels in other Greek cities.

Alexander also briefly considered punishing various Greek leaders suspected of aiding the Theban insurrection. He changed his mind after receiving a visit from the Athenian statesman-general Phocion, a man widely respected for his honesty, courage, and sense of duty. In his biography of Phocion, Plutarch recorded the meeting, saying,

> Alexander not only consented to receive Phocion and hear his petition, but he actually listened to his advice, which was as follows. If it was peace that Alexander wanted above all, then he should make an end of the fighting, but if it was glory, then he should transfer the theater of war and turn his arms away from Greece against the barbarians. Phocion spoke at length and his words were well chosen to fit Alexander's character and aspirations, with the result that he quite transformed the king's mood.[3]

Alexander was mightily impressed with Phocion, in whose bold and stalwart character he may have sensed a kindred spirit. Athens once more escaped damage and occupation by Macedonian troops.

Alexander's Conquests

In the following year, 334 B.C., having been confirmed the new captain-general of the Hellenic League, Alexander turned his attention to the larger goal his father had set three years earlier—the invasion of Persia. The young king's legendary campaigns in Asia began when he crossed the Hellespont with an army of about thirty-two thousand infantry. Of these troops, some twelve thousand were Macedonians, composing the phalanx. Another fourteen thousand were hoplites and peltasts from league member states. The other six thousand were archers and peltasts from Thrace and the southern Aegean island of Crete. The army also had about five thousand cavalry, consisting of two thousand of the Macedonian King's Companions, eighteen hundred expert Thessalian horsemen, and a mixture of smaller Thracian and allied contingents. This was Greece's first true unified army.

The new army's first test came just weeks after it had crossed the Hellespont. At the Granicus River in Asia Minor, Alexander won a victory over a slightly larger enemy force. He then marched south. In 333, at Issus, just south of Asia Minor, his forces met a Persian Army, commanded by Darius III, the Persian king himself. Estimates by ancient historians for the

Source Document

Alexander sent him a present of a hundred talents. When this arrived in Athens, Phocion asked those who brought it why . . . Alexander should have singled out him as the recipient of such a huge sum. They answered, "Because Alexander considers that only you are a good and honorable man." Phocion's reply was, "In that case let him allow me to continue in that state and to enjoy that reputation always." But when the messengers followed him to his house and saw his frugal way of life, how his wife kneaded the bread, while Phocion with his own hands drew water from the well . . . they were indignant and pressed him even more to accept the money: they exclaimed that it was monstrous that Phocion, who was an honored friend of the king, should live in such poverty. Phocion caught sight of a poor old man who was walking by dressed in a squalid cloak, and so he asked them which of the two they thought inferior, himself or the old man. . . . "This man has less to live on than I have [said Phocion], and yet he finds it quite enough. In other words . . . either I make no use of this enormous sum, or if I do, I shall destroy my good name with the Athenians and with the king as well." So the treasure went back . . . after it had served to prove to the Greeks that the man who did not need such a sum was richer than the man who had offered it.[4]

Plutarch recorded this famous and charming footnote to the friendship that developed between the Athenian statesman Phocion and Macedonia's young king, Alexander.

size of the Persian force range from two hundred fifty thousand to six hundred thousand. However, these are certainly exaggerated. A more realistic figure would be one hundred thousand to one hundred fifty thousand, about three times the size of the Greek force. Though greatly outnumbered, the Greeks proved their superiority in armor, training, and strategy. As the Persian lines began to crumble, the terrified Darius decided to get away while he could, as described in Arrian's *Anabasis*:

> The moment the Persian left went to pieces under Alexander's attack and Darius, in his war chariot, saw that it was cut off, he . . . fled—indeed, he led the race for safety. Keeping to his chariot as long as there was smooth ground to travel on, he was forced to abandon it when ravines and other obstructions barred his way; then, dropping his shield and stripping off his mantle—and even leaving his bow in the war chariot—he leapt upon a horse and rode for his life.[5]

After this major victory, Alexander seemed almost invincible. In 332, he continued south and liberated Egypt, which had been under Persian rule for two centuries. In the Nile Delta, he founded a new city, Alexandria (named after himself, of course). It soon became one of the ancient world's greatest commercial and cultural centers. Its culture was particularly important in the long run. Here, as he would continue to do in the later stages of his conquest, Alexander introduced Greek language, arts, ideas, and customs. In this Hellenization process, Greek and local cultures often combined to form new

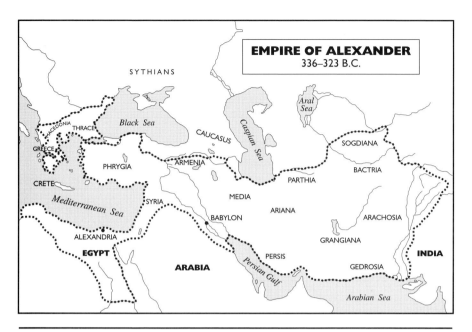

EMPIRE OF ALEXANDER
336–323 B.C.

Alexander set out to expand the empire his father had built by conquering cultures beyond Greece.

and exotic Hellenistic, or "Greek-like," versions. For this reason, historians refer to the roughly three-century-long period following Alexander's campaigns as the Hellenistic Age.

Having departed Egypt and marched into the heart of Persia, in October 331, Alexander again soundly defeated Darius, this time at Gaugamela, near the Tigris River in modern-day Iraq. In this battle, which forever decided Persia's fate, at least forty thousand Persians were killed. The Greeks lost fewer than a thousand men. Darius again panicked and fled, only to be murdered by his own officers shortly afterward.

Not satisfied with subduing the greatest empire the world had yet known, Alexander pushed farther east, establishing new cities and military outposts as he went. Eventually, in 326, he reached India. At the Hydaspes River, he promptly defeated a large Indian Army that included two hundred battle elephants, then a frightening novelty in warfare. At this point, the young king's exhausted troops, most of whom had not seen home in years, demanded that he turn back. He was forced to do so but believed it only a temporary delay in his schedule for further conquests. However, the delay turned out to be a permanent one. As if confirming his own prediction that his life would be short, Alexander died at age thirty-three,

Alexander was able to defeat a large Indian Army, despite the Indians' use of battle elephants.

Source Document

The elephant-drivers forced their beasts to meet the opposing cavalry, while the Macedonian infantry, in its turn, advanced against them, shooting down the drivers, and pouring in a hail of missiles from every side upon the elephants themselves. It was an odd bit of work—quite unlike any previous battle; the monster elephants plunged this way and that among the lines of infantry, dealing destruction . . . and as they blundered about . . . they trampled to death as many of their friends as of their enemies. The result was that the Indian cavalry, jammed in around the elephants and with no more space to maneuvre than they had, suffered severely. . . . Riderless and bewildered . . . and maddened by pain and fear, [the beasts ran amok], thrusting, trampling, and spreading death before them.[6]

Battle elephants were a novelty at the time of Alexander the Great. This description of Alexander's men fighting the huge creatures at the Battle of Hydaspes in 326 B.C. is from Arrian's Anabasis.

possibly of malaria, in Persia in June 323. As Philip had died in Greece, never to see Asia, his son now perished in Asia, never to return to Greece.

The Successor Kingdoms

Alexander had carved out a vast empire stretching from Macedonia to western India and containing hundreds of diverse local peoples and cultures. But this immense realm barely outlived its creator. Almost immediately after Alexander was gone, his leading generals began fighting over who should succeed him. Accordingly, these ambitious men became known as the *Diadochoi*, or "Successors." Their desperate contest to win an empire did not produce a clear victor, however. The problem was that there were so many of them—at least thirty-four at the outset—and nearly all were more or less evenly matched in determination and military prowess.

As the fighting raged on and Alexander's empire began to fragment, the field narrowed. A few of the *Diadochoi*, along with their sons—who became known as the *Epigoni*, or "those born after"— emerged as the principal leaders after a series of devastating wars. Among these were Antigonus, called "the One-Eyed," his son Demetrius, who became known as Poliorcetes, or "the Besieger;" Ptolemy, who seized Egypt; Antipater and his son Cassander, both of whom fought for control of Macedonia and Greece; Lysimachus, who for a while lorded over Thrace; and Seleucus, who battled to

Source Document

[They had] a square base, each side of which measured seventy-two feet at the bottom. [They were] ninety-nine feet high with the upper parts tapering off to narrower dimensions. Inside . . . [each] was divided into many separate stories and compartments . . . and it was manned with troops who were equipped with every kind of weapon.[7]

Demetrius, son of Alexander's general Antigonus, earned the nickname "The Besieger" for his use of massive siege machines and mechanical weapons. Plutarch described Demetrius's famous siege towers.

gain control over the western parts of the old Persian realm. Clearly, the Greek unity to which Philip had devoted his career and given his life had disintegrated into a bloody state of anarchy.

After over forty years of incessant wars, by about 280 B.C., the borders of three major Hellenistic kingdoms had taken more or less permanent shape. The Ptolemaic kingdom, ruled by Ptolemy's successors, consisted of Egypt and nearby southern Palestine. The Seleucid kingdom, led by Seleucus's descendants, encompassed what is now Iran and Iraq and part of

Alexander the Great died at the age of thirty-three, failing to conquer Asia. This modern drawing depicts his funeral procession.

Asia Minor. And the Macedonian kingdom, ruled by the Antigonids, the family line of Antigonus, consisted of the old Macedonia, Thrace, and Greece. These large monarchies, historian Chester G. Starr explained,

> were not firmly united territorial states, as the Greek city-states had been; rather, they were held together by the political and military abilities of the kings of the three major [family] lines. This situation in itself led to wars to secure the necessary prestige for survival. . . . Throughout the third century [B.C.] the Ptolemies generally held the upper hand, not so much because their armies were efficient as because they were masters of the sea and had tremendous financial resources through their exploitation of Egypt. Yet the Hellenistic statesmen understood fairly well the principle of the balance of power, and so other major and minor states tended to unite

against any dynasty which seemed overly powerful. Treaties of alliance [and] of dynastic marriage . . . succeeded one another in the ever-shifting lines of diplomatic activity much as in eighteenth-century Europe.[8]

Thus, after hundreds of thousands of people had died and whole regions had been devastated in the ruinous *Diadochoi* wars, the rivalry and destruction continued in periodic clashes among the Hellenistic realms. Years before, the disunity of the Greeks in the city-states had left them open to conquest by a stronger outside power, namely Macedonia. Now history was about to repeat itself—the Hellenistic Greeks' persistent failure to get along condemned them to an identical fate.

The Eagle's Wings

During these years of ceaseless bickering among Hellenistic rulers in Asia and the eastern Mediterranean, a new power had been rising in that sea's western sphere. The small city-state of Rome had begun many centuries before as a backward farming community on the Tiber River near the west-central Italian coast. Its rise to greatness began in 509 B.C., when its chief landowners, partly inspired by reports of democratic doings in distant Athens, threw out their king and established the Roman Republic. Though not a true democracy, the republic did feature some elements of representative government, including legislative assemblies and elections to choose most leaders. Hardy, courageous, fiercely patriotic, and imbued (as Alexander had been) with the notion that they had a divine destiny to conquer and rule others, Roman armies marched steadily outward from their homeland. By 265, they had taken control of all of Italy. By 201, after two devastating wars with the maritime empire of Carthage, centered in northern Africa, the Romans were masters of the whole western Mediterranean.

Now an imperialistic power of the first magnitude, Rome immediately turned toward the sea's eastern sphere and the large but war-weary and weak Hellenistic kingdoms. Few Greeks recognized the seriousness of the threat. Only a handful of orators stood up and called on their fellow Greeks to unite in the cause of freedom and security for all—as had Gorgias and Isocrates of old. In 213 B.C., even before the Romans had finished off Carthage, the orator Agelaus of Aetolia delivered this warning:

> It would be best of all if the Greeks never made war upon each other, but . . . [could] speak with one heart and voice, and marching arm and arm like men fording a river, repel barbarian invaders and unite in preserving themselves and their cities. . . . For it is evident that whether the Carthaginians beat the Romans or the Romans the Carthaginians . . . it is not in the least likely that the victors will be content with . . . Italy and Sicily, but they are sure to come here and extend their ambitions beyond the bounds of justice.[9]

As in the past, the Greeks ignored this and similar pleas for unity and quickly paid the price. In the next century and a half, the Greek states fell one by one

This excellent Roman copy of an original Greek bust of Alexander, probably as he appeared in his twenties, is presently on display in the Archaeological Museum at Thessaloniki.

before the might of Rome. On September 2, 31 B.C., the last of the Hellenistic monarchs, Cleopatra VII of the Ptolemaic kingdom—who had become embroiled in a Roman civil war—suffered defeat at Actium in western Greece, and Egypt became a Roman province. The outstretched wings of the Roman eagle (Rome's national symbol) now spanned the whole Mediterranean, which the Romans had arrogantly come to call *mare nostrum*, "our sea."

Over several centuries, Greece had produced many great artists, thinkers, and leaders, but only Philip and Alexander ever fully grasped the importance of unity or possessed the strength and determination needed to forge it. Philip had made the dream of Panhellenism a reality. From him, Alexander and his successors had inherited the vision, political structure, and army needed to enforce it. Had these successors imitated Alexander and tried to preserve what Philip had created, a united and powerful Greece may have been able to withstand the Roman onslaught and history would have been very different.

Yet the Greeks' failure to get along with one another was hardly a fault unique to them. In succeeding ages, people and nations repeatedly failed to learn the lessons of the past. They fought among themselves and had to rediscover again and again the advantages of unity. Philip and Alexander could, with extraordinary skill, conquer human beings and their works, but they could not, after all, change human nature.

Timeline

480 B.C.—The Persian Empire launches a massive attack on Greece; The Greeks temporarily unite under Athens and Sparta and by the end of 479 successfully expel the invaders, but hostility between Greece and Persia is destined to carry on for the next century and a half.

437—Athens, at the height of its power, wealth, and influence, establishes the city of Amphipolis on the northern Aegean coast.

431 –404—All of the Greek city-states are devastated or exhausted by the massive Peloponnesian War, which ends when Athens surrenders to Sparta; This begins Sparta's domination of Greece.

ca. 410 –405—Macedonia's King Archelaus relocates his kingdom's capital from Aegae to Pella, hoping to move his country into the Greek economic and cultural mainstream.

394—Sparta, under King Agesilaus, defeats Athens and Thebes at Coronea in western Boeotia, ensuring Sparta's continued dominance.

392—In a speech delivered at the Olympic Games, the Greek orator Gorgias calls for the Greek city-states to unite in a war against Persia, a plea that goes largely unheeded.

ca. 382—Philip II, future king of Macedonia, is born.

380—The Greek orator Isocrates publishes his *Panegyricus*, advocating a united Greek anti-Persian crusade.

371—Under its brilliant General Epaminondas, Thebes defeats Sparta at Leuctra in Boeotia, destroying the myth of Spartan invincibility and initiating Theban domination of Greek affairs.

368—The teenage Philip begins his three-year stay as a hostage in Thebes, where he is exposed to Theban military methods.

359—Philip becomes king of Macedonia after his older brother is killed in battle.

357—After uniting his fragmented kingdom, Philip seizes the important commercial port of Amphipolis; Athens fails to intervene.

356—Philip's son Alexander III, who will later be called "Alexander the Great," is born.

353—Philip defeats the Phocians from southern Greece, who have occupied the central Greek region of Thessaly; He then proceeds to occupy Thessaly himself.

351—The great Athenian orator Demosthenes, so far one of the few important Greek public figures to recognize that Philip is a dangerous threat to the southern city-states, delivers the first of his anti-Philip speeches—the *Philippics*.

348—After a long siege, Philip takes Olynthus, the leading city of the Chalcidian peninsula in the northwestern Aegean.

346—Envoys from Athens, including Demosthenes, strike a deal with Philip designed to contain his aggressions; Ignoring the agreement, Philip boldly moves through the strategic pass of Thermopylae, on Thessaly's southeastern border, defeats the Phocians in their own territory, and takes control of the sacred sanctuary at Delphi; Isocrates publishes his *Address to Philip*, calling on him to champion Greece against Persia.

344—Demosthenes delivers his *Second Philippic*.

ca. **343 –342**—Philip consolidates his northern conquests by subduing central and northern Thrace and turning that kingdom into a Macedonian province.

ca. **342**—Alexander begins studying with the noted philosopher-scientist Aristotle.

341—Demosthenes gives his *Third Philippic*.

338—Demosthenes forges an anti-Macedonian alliance headed by Athens and Thebes; Philip, aided by Alexander, defeats the Greek allies at Chaeronea in western Boeotia, beginning Macedonia's domination of Greece; Philip presides over the first meeting of the Congress of Corinth, in which he imposes a Macedonian-controlled federal union on the Greek states.

337—Philip announces his plans for a united Greek crusade against Persia at the second meeting of the congress; He also divorces Olympias, Alexander's mother, and marries a Macedonian maiden.

336—Philip is assassinated by a Macedonian, and twenty-year-old Alexander succeeds him as king.

334—Alexander launches an invasion of Persia, fulfilling the goal earlier set by his father; The Greeks decisively defeat the Persians at the Granicus River in northwestern Asia Minor.

331—Alexander defeats Persian King Darius III at Gaugamela in modern-day Iraq, effectively eliminating Persia's power to resist.

326—Alexander and his men reach India, defeat a large Indian Army, and then turn back into Persia.

323—Alexander dies in Persia at age thirty-three.

323 –280—Alexander's generals and their sons battle each other for dominance in a series of devastating wars that shatter the Greek unity Philip and his own son had worked so hard to achieve and maintain; Eventually, three large kingdoms emerge from the wreckage of Alexander's empire—the Ptolemaic, Seleucid, and Macedonian; These realms subsequently fight among themselves, growing weaker and becoming vulnerable to domination by the rising power of Rome.

31—Ptolemaic Egypt's Queen Cleopatra VII, last of the Greek rulers descended from Philip and Alexander's generals, is defeated while fighting in a Roman civil war; Egypt becomes a Roman province, ending independent Greek rule in the Mediterranean world.

Chapter Notes

Chapter 1.   The Elusive Dream of Greek Unity

1. M. B. Sakellariou, "Panhellenism: From Concept to Policy," in Miltiades B. Hatzopoulos and Louisa D. Loukopoulos, eds., *Philip of Macedon* (Athens: Ekdotike Athenon, 1980), p. 128.

2. Isocrates, *Panegyricus*, quoted in Paul J. Alexander, ed., *The Ancient World: To 300 A.D.* (New York: Macmillan, 1963), p. 161.

Chapter 2.   An Inability to Get Along

1. Quoted in Thucydides, *The Peloponnesian War*, trans. Rex Warner (New York: Penguin Books), p. 148.

2. Peter Connolly, *The Greek Armies* (Morristown, N.J.: Silver Burdett, 1979), p. 26.

3. Xenophon, *A History of My Times*, trans. Rex Warner (New York: Penguin Books, 1979), pp. 204–205.

4. Ibid., pp. 219–220.

5. Plutarch, *Life of Pelopidas*, in Ian Scott-Kilvert, trans., *Plutarch: The Age of Alexander* (New York: Penguin Books, 1973), p. 90.

6. Diodorus Siculus, *Library of History*, trans. Charles L. Sherman (Cambridge, Mass.: Harvard University Press, 1963), vol. 7, pp. 107–111.

7. Plutarch, p. 93.

Chapter 3.   An Overlord Among Equals

1. Peter Green, *Alexander of Macedon, 356–323 B.C.: A Historical Biography* (Berkeley: University of California Press, 1991), p. 7.

2. Herodotus, *The Histories*, trans. Aubrey de Sélincourt (New York: Penguin Books, 1972), pp. 347–348, 571–572.

3. Green, pp. 24–25.

4. J. R. Ellis, "The Unification of Macedonia," in Miltiades B. Hatzopoulos and Louisa D. Loukopoulos, eds., *Philip of Macedon* (Athens: Ekdotike Athenon, 1980), p. 42.

5. Arrian, *Anabasis Alexandri*, published as *The Campaigns of Alexander*, trans. Aubrey de Sélincourt (New York: Penguin Books, 1971), pp. 360–361.

6. David G. Hogarth, *Philip and Alexander of Macedon* (Freeport, N.Y.: Books for the Libraries Press, 1971), p. 3.

Chapter 4.   Warrior, Diplomat, and Schemer

1. J. B. Bury, *A History of Greece to the Death of Alexander,* rev. Russell Meiggs (London: Macmillan, 1975), pp. 688–689.

2. Diodorus Siculus, *Library of History*, trans. C. Bradford Welles (Cambridge, Mass.: Harvard University Press, 1963), vol. 8, p. 103.

3. J. R. Ellis, *Philip II and Macedonian Imperialism* (New York: Thames and Hudson, 1977), p. 66.

4. Diodorus Siculus, vol. 7, p. 315.

5. Demosthenes, *First Philippic*, in *Olynthiacs, Philippics, Minor Speeches*, trans. J. H. Vince (Cambridge, Mass.: Harvard University Press, 1962), pp. 73–75.

6. Demosthenes, *Second Olynthiac*, in Vince, p. 27; *Third Olynthiac*, in Vince, p. 51.

7. Plutarch, *Life of Demosthenes*, in Ian Scott-Kilvert, trans., *Plutarch: The Age of Alexander* (New York: Penguin Books, 1973), p. 203.

8. Isocrates, *Address to Philip*, in Paul J. Alexander, ed., *The Ancient World: To 300 A.D.* (New York: Macmillan, 1963), p. 171.

Chapter 5. To Decide the Fate of Greece

1. Demosthenes, *Second Philippic*, in *Olynthiacs, Philippics, Minor Speeches*, trans. J. H. Vince (Cambridge, Mass.: Harvard University Press, 1962), pp. 141–143.

2. Plutarch, *Life of Alexander*, in Ian Scott-Kilvert, trans., *Plutarch: The Age of Alexander* (New York: Penguin Books, 1973), pp. 259–260.

3. Ibid., p. 256.

4. Plutarch, *Life of Demosthenes*, in Scott-Kilvert, p. 204.

5. Peter Green, *Alexander of Macedon, 356–323 B.C.: A Historical Biography* (Berkeley: University of California Press, 1991), pp. 73–74.

6. Ibid., p. 75.

7. Plutarch, *Life of Demosthenes*, p. 205.

8. Plutarch, *Life of Pelopidas*, in Scott-Kilvert, pp. 85–86.

Chapter 6. A Vision of the Future

1. George Cawkwell, "Philip and Athens," in Miltiades B. Hatzopoulos and Louisa D. Loukopoulos, eds., *Philip of Macedon* (Athens: Ekdotike Athenon, 1980), p. 110.

2. M. B. Sakellariou, "Panhellenism: From Concept to Policy," in Hatzopoulos and Loukopoulos, p. 135.

3. Peter Green, *Alexander of Macedon, 356–323 B.C.: A Historical Biography* (Berkeley: University of California Press, 1991), p. 86.

4. N.G.L. Hammond, *Philip of Macedon* (Baltimore: Johns Hopkins University Press, 1994), p. 207.

5. Eugene N. Borza, *In the Shadow of Olympus: The Emergence of Macedon* (Princeton, N.J.: Princeton University Press, 1990), p. 226.

6. Plutarch, *Life of Alexander*, in Ian Scott-Kilvert, trans., *Plutarch: The Age of Alexander* (New York: Penguin Books, 1973), p. 261.

7. Diodorus Siculus, *Library of History*, trans. C. Bradford Welles (Cambridge, Mass.: Harvard University Press, 1963), vol. 8, pp. 95, 99–101.

8. Plutarch, *Life of Demosthenes*, in Scott-Kilvert, p. 207.

Chapter 7. The Inheritors of a Vision

1. Plutarch, *Life of Alexander*, in Ian Scott-Kilvert, trans., *Plutarch: The Age of Alexander* (New York: Penguin Books, 1973), pp. 255–256.

2. Arrian, *Anabasis*, 5.26, Don Nardo, trans.; see also Arrian, *Anabasis Alexandri*, published as *The Campaigns of Alexander*, trans. Aubrey de Sélincourt (New York: Penguin Books, 1971), p. 294.

3. Plutarch, *Life of Phocion*, in Scott-Kilvert, pp. 232–233.

4. Ibid., pp. 233–234.

5. Arrian, *Anabasis*, in *The Campaigns of Alexander*, p. 120.

6. Arrian, *Anabasis Alexandri*, in *The Campaigns of Alexander*, pp. 278–279.

7. Plutarch, *Life of Demetrius*, in Scott-Kilvert, p. 352.

8. Chester G. Starr, *A History of the Ancient World* (New York: Oxford University Press, 1991), pp. 404–405.

9. Agelaus of Aetolia, quoted in Polybius, *The Histories*, trans. W. R. Paton (Cambridge Mass.: Harvard University Press, 1966), vol. 5, p. 103.

Further Reading

Books

Asimov, Isaac. *Greeks: A Great Adventure*. Boston: Houghton Mifflin, 1965.

Connolly, Peter. *The Greek Armies*. Morristown, N.J.: Silver Burdett Press, 1979.

Hendricks, Rhonda A., trans. *Classical Gods and Heroes*. New York: Morrow Quill, 1974.

Léveque, Pierre. *The Birth of Greece*. New York: Harry N. Abrams, 1994.

MacDonald, Fiona. *The World in the Time of Alexander the Great*. Morristown, N.J.: Silver Burdett Press, 1997.

Nardo, Don. *The Age of Pericles*. San Diego: Lucent Books, 1996.

———. *The Battle of Marathon*. San Diego: Lucent Books, 1996.

———. *Cleopatra*. San Diego: Lucent Books, 1994.

———. *Life in Ancient Athens*. San Diego: Lucent Books, 2000.

———. *The Parthenon*. San Diego: Lucent Books, 1999.

———. *The Persian Empire*. San Diego: Lucent Books, 1998.

Peach, Susan, and Anne Millard. *The Greeks*. London: Usborne, 1990.

Theule, Frederic. *Alexander & His Times*. New York: Henry Holt & Company, 1995.

Internet Addresses

Alexander the Great History Project. 1997. <http://www.hackneys.com/alex_web/index.htm>.

Ancient Sites: The Ancient History Community. 1999. <http://www.thevines.com/leaf/AA172989>.

Fenton, Joshua. "Philip II, King of Macedon." *David's Ancient World*. April 1998. <http://members.tripod.com/~Kekrops/Hellenistic_Files/Philip_2.html>.

Stevenson, Daniel C. "Alexander by Plutarch." *The Internet Classics Archive*. <http://classics.mit.edu/Plutarch/alexandr.html>.

Index